Learn How To Create A Safe Working Environment For Your Team

SHAKRUDDIN KHAN

Published by SHAKRUDDIN KHAN, 2024.

While every precaution has been taken in the preparation of this book, the publisher assumes no responsibility for errors or omissions, or for damages resulting from the use of the information contained herein.

LEARN HOW TO CREATE A SAFE WORKING ENVIRONMENT FOR YOUR TEAM

First edition. February 26, 2024.

Copyright © 2024 SHAKRUDDIN KHAN.

ISBN: 979-8224367795

Written by SHAKRUDDIN KHAN.

Also by SHAKRUDDIN KHAN

The Smart Way To Personal Finance Success
Goal Setting 101 Achieve More Goals Than Ever! Faster!
Blockchain Masterclass for Businesses and Corporations
Master Your Mindset & Brain Framestorm Your Way To Success
Manipulation Techniques: How Can We Influence People's Thoughts And Behaviors
Leadership How To Influence, Inspire And Impact As A Leader
Learn How To Create A Safe Working Environment For Your Team

Table of Contents

Copyright

Learn How To Create A Safe Working Environment For Your Team

Book Design by **SHAKRUDDIN KHAN**

About

Are you trying to improve your team's success despite lots of conflict and organizational issues around them? Do you wish you had practical steps that can help you insulate them from all the politics? Do you just need some practical steps about what you can do to protect your team from outside interference so that they can get on with their job?

In this Book you will learn practical ways in which you can improve the psychological safety of your team environment. Learn from international best practice research about why this matters and how you can achieve your goals.

This Book is the result of a study of agile teams around the world as well as the experience I have gained in running small teams and projects for over 20 years. You'll get the practical and insights you need to improve your team environment and help your team be more successful. I look forward to seeing you in the Book.

Introduction

Hello and welcome to this conflict resolution Book here. We are going to cover everything related to identifying conflicts, dealing with conflicts, not falling into the usual traps of conflicts in personal life, professional life, and many other scenarios. Let's take a moment just to review what are the goals for this Book. Welcome to the Conflict Resolution chapter. In this chapter, we are going to learn how to properly de-escalate and resolve conflicts and tense situations with others in order to achieve a common goal. In terms of goals, our major goal in this chapter is to effectively address and resolve conflicts.

That's what we're here for. But more specifically in detail, we are going to learn how to assess the different conflict types grouped into hot and cold as well as the specific breach of rules that caused the conflict in the first place. How to properly calm down and empathize with the other person or mediate conflicts between two third parties? How to avoid the common traps that cause an escalation of the situation, such as disrespecting or belittling the other side? How to avoid misalignment traps that will cause other conflicts later, such as not aligning expectations or promising things that you can't deliver.

And finally, how to properly support and comfort others when they are in an emotional state, for example, among other things. In order to achieve this, we are going to focus on three different dimensions of conflicts, three families of techniques, if you will. The first is the diagnostic, properly assessing what type of conflict you have on your hands, as well as what led up to it in the first place.

Then actual techniques to use empathy, focusing on implementation, personal boundaries and others that actually help you solve the conflict. And finally, we'll take a look at traps, both in terms of mismatches in expectations, but also escalation traps that can make a situation much worse. So as we see in this Book, we are going to go all the way from identifying a conflict in the beginning to using specific tools to actually fix it and not fall into the traps along the way.

Let's talk about the diagnostic in this group of topics. We are going to cover how to identify what type of conflict you have on our hands and if possible, what caused it in the first place. Let's cover this group of topics before handling a conflict. It's crucial to properly analyze what type of conflict it is and what led to it in the first place. Because although the techniques used to deal with the conflict will be mostly the same, knowing what triggered it and what type of conflict it actually is, is important at least to know how to prevent it in the future by addressing the specific trigger.

Two things that are essential to know at this diagnostic stage are both how the people are actually behaving, the different types of reactions, hot or cold conflicts, and also what rule violations cause the conflict in the first place. Because every conflict means that somebody had a rule and somebody else violated that rule. In order to cover this initial diagnostic phase, we are then going to focus on these two key areas. The first is the types of conflicts, the types of reactions that people may have. Avoiding being aggressive, withdrawing, poisoning others, being passive aggressive and more. Then we'll take a look at the specific rules that people have that cause a conflict when they are broken and how to adapt to them to avoid them in the future.

It's important to know that these rules may be reasonable or not. For example, a person may have a rule of every time that someone raises their voice, I feel disrespected, which may be reasonable, but another person may have a rule of every time that someone questions me, even if they're right, I feel disrespected, which may not be that easy to justify. So as you see in this group of topics, we are going to cover what type of conflict we have on our hands as well as what caused it.

Conflict Types

Let's talk about conflict types. Usually not all conflicts are made equal and people can have one of two attitudes related to a conflict. So let's cover what are these two types of conflicts as well as the indicated techniques to fix each one of these. When a conflict does break out, people can have many different reactions. It's funny that when you think of conflict, you probably think of two people arguing loudly over each other, a shouting match. But in reality, conflicts come in many shapes and sizes, and all of them, make no mistake, must be considered conflicts. Someone avoiding something, being passive aggressive or others are all forms of conflict, and the way to deal with this is also mostly the same.

But nevertheless, it's important to realize the different types of conflict that you may be dealing with. One possibility is that the person may just outright avoid the issue, pretend that it didn't happen or pretend to agree just to move on false compliance. Another possibility is that the person may borrow things constantly. We become more and more stressed and possibly once they can take it anymore, they eventually blow up in your face. Another possibility is that the person may become more aggressive, even being verbally abusive or just taking an accusatory stance. Being defensive, or another possibility is that they may become passive aggressive, sabotaging things on purpose to make their point without a direct confrontation or even poisoning other people behind the scenes.

Despite the different types of reactions, these can usually be grouped in a very broad sense into hot or cold conflicts. Hot conflicts are the ones based on too much intensity, aggressiveness, insults, verbal abuse. It's what you probably think of when you think of a conflict called conflicts are the ones based on a lack of communication. So passive aggressiveness, voluntarily withdrawing, avoiding the topic, even becoming delusional and ignoring the facts or pretending that everything is fine. All fit is a pattern. While the general way to address both of these is usually the same. And we're going to take a look at it, including techniques such as applying empathy, showing respect, making the person feel understood, and trying to reach an equitable conclusion for both sides.

It's important to add an extra layer of understanding in hot conflicts so that you can slowly calm down an aggressive person and bring them back down to the realm of logic so that the reasonable in for code conflicts to proactively stimulate communication because the person is going to withdraw and you need to be the one to slowly bring them out. What are some implementation pointers in terms of the different conflict types? The first is objectivity. Despite the type of conflict, remaining objective is always essential. If the other side feels disrespected, ignored or victimized in some way, things will get worse.

And in many cases they already do this even if you are objective. So if you're not, it will be even worse. The second is that people can have wild swings. People usually do have one pattern, some just avoid, some just become aggressive and so on. Sure. But it is possible for people to swing wildly. For example, someone very aggressive can be put in their place and in the future they don't speak their mind anymore because they're stubborn or they're pouting. But on the other hand, someone with a cold conflict that is withdrawn and is borrowing things up and doesn't speak up may end up blowing up and becoming very aggressive when they actually can't take it anymore.

Diagnosing is crucial as people can have so many different reactions. It's important to assess the ones they may have when something may be wrong with them, there may be a conflict there. And finally, remember that all of these types are conflicts. Conflicts are not just when people are aggressive and in each other's faces. All of these types are conflicts and should be taken seriously. Worrisome do's and don'ts of the different conflict types. DOS do have that weird awkward conversation to really figure out what may be wrong with someone. It's better to have a small conflict now than let it grow and have a bigger one later. Don't assume that code conflicts are not conflicts behind every attitude of withdrawing and avoiding.

There is a reason and chances are this situation could have been fixed. What are some examples of the different conflict types? The first is a screaming match. Again, it's probably what you think of when you think of a conflict. Two people being aggressive, shouting in each other's face. It's not the only type, but it is a type. Another example is someone being passive aggressive. They don't fight the other person openly. They poison a. People behind your back or they sabotage what the person wants to do. Make no mistake, this is a type of conflict as well. And finally, avoidance.

When someone avoids a person or a topic that they just don't want to deal with, that is a conflict. They may be trying to avoid the confrontation, ironically, but avoidance itself is a type of conflict. What are our key takeaways here? The first is that there are multiple types of conflict. Everyone deals with things in their own way. So conflict comes in many shapes and sizes. But all of these are conflicts and all of them must be handled usually in the same way. Then the different types of conflicts can be broadly grouped into hot and cold ones. While hot conflicts are about aggressiveness and intensity, conflicts are about avoidance and withdrawal.

And remember that you can find all key takeaways on the key takeaways wiki page, both the link and the password are in the Book description for convenience so that you can just copy and paste them. So as we see, we usually have two types of conflicts: hot and cold. If it's a hot

8

conflict, then the person is very emotional and you want them to calm down using empathy. If it's a cold conflict, then they're not speaking their mind and you want them to slowly speak up more and more and tell you what they will be thinking.

Conflict Types in Financial Services

Although we're going to use similar techniques in both cases, it's always helpful to diagnose whether you have a hot or cold conflict on your hands in a hot conflict. The other side will be very angry, screaming at you, name calling, lashing out or similar, very aggressive, very in your face in a court conflict. The other side will kind of withdraw and not say what they really think. They can wait or be cynical or passive aggressive or just feel emotionally offended or hurt while you solve both cases in mostly the same way. Remember that for hot conflicts, the goal is to empathize and show understanding with a person as they slowly calm down during four hot conflicts. You want to persist to get the person to speak their mind. You want to kind of warm them up until they're comfortable saying what they really think.

Rule Analysis and Adaptation

Let's talk about rule analysis and adaptation. There is every single time that you have a conflict because you broke someone's rules, whether they're spoken or unspoken. For example, with a client. Maybe you actually provided a bad service, but maybe you just disrespect them. You need to know what somebody's rules are, because if you don't know what you broke, you can avoid breaking it in the future. Let's take a look at how rules work. As we mentioned, all conflicts come from a person triggering another one by breaking one of the rules. And these can be very generic or very specific, very explicit, depending on the person. And for some pairs of people, these can actually be in direct conflict. Let me give you some examples.

I may have an implicit rule of if you interrupt me when I'm speaking, I will feel disrespected. On the other hand, you may have a rule that it's okay to interrupt everybody else and they can interrupt me as well. You can see how these two rules can create a conflict between these two people, especially if each side is not aware that the other side has an opposing rule. This can degenerate very quickly, or I may have an implicit rule of if you market yourself and you publicize yourself with no results, you're not really authentic. While the other side may have a rule, it's important to draw attention to yourself above all others at all costs and then deliver value. You can see how these two people can crash very easily.

And again, it will be even worse if they're not aware of each other's rules. So whenever a conflict occurs, it's important to diagnose what rules each side has for being disrespected so that you can identify which one was broken for each side. Possibly only one side. This allows each side to respect the other side's rules once they are clarified. Apologize for having broken down. If that's the case, find a compromise in the future. Now, here's the thing. In some cases the rule is obvious. You can ask somebody why their colleague disrespected them and they'll say openly, Well, he called me an idiot. The case is pretty clear cut. And you know who needs to change their behavior to avoid these conflicts in the future? But in some cases, it's going to be more subtle.

It can be because someone assumed something or someone did something that would not always be wrong, but in specific circumstances is, for example, someone taking a lead in a project without explicitly having been assigned the leader and without having validated this with the other people in the group. Or, for example, someone taking the lead when there is a superior present that is being overtaken in a way. In this case, the solution is always to ask questions, to find out, ask people what in specific made them feel angry or upset or broke the rules and slowly uncover what the original trigger was, as well as the person's behavior leading up to it? What are some implementation pointers in terms of uncovering and adapting to people's rules? First, realize that compromise is necessary In many cases.

There are situations where the rules are simply incompatible. For example, if you have an introvert that only speaks when others are done speaking and an extrovert that will keep on speaking and hammering until they are interrupted. In those cases, both people need to change. Remember that as with many things in life, this is a process and covering a rule and getting a commitment from someone that they will adapt is not going to magically fix things. It's the beginning of a process and there can be some subsequent bumps in the road until you're in the clear. A fourth point is to take into account the company culture. Does a specific rule go against the company culture? For example, being an introvert is perfectly fine, but if you are in a department where people solve crises, you must intervene quickly and take action.

If someone does not voice their opinion quickly and wait too long, that rule can actually go against the expected behaviors and culture of the company or their team at least. And finally, remember that people lie. Take what they say with a grain of salt. In some cases, people just snap. And there was no particular rule broken. In some cases, someone felt offended. But the other side then really offended them or someone was provoked. But the other side conveniently forgets to mention the provocation. Don't be too quick to force specific people to take specific behaviors until it's clear why this conflict really occurred. What are some do's and don'ts in terms of analyzing and adapting to rules do's? Do try to clarify as much as possible.

If the rule isn't clear, you don't have a rule. I just felt that being defensive was worth it. I feel offended when someone calls me incompetent is much better. Don'ts. Don't consider rules absolute when the rule is ridiculous. By all means, request a change. Rules like I feel disrespected if people don't support my opinion and don't use it in every case are not just unreasonable, they are plain crazy. In these cases you have to prove to the person that they are the ones who must change. What are some examples of rules? The first is people that have a rule, others not raising their voice. I can have a rule dictating that if you raise your voice, this conversation is over and I may even decide to leave. This can be a completely reasonable rule.

Someone may have a rule of others not questioning them under any circumstance. If anyone dares to challenge what they have to say, even in a polite manner, the person will become defensive or aggressive. This one is not that reasonable and not that easy to justify. And finally, someone may have a rule of others not going behind your back. They want to act as the gatekeeper for all information and not allow other people to speak among themselves. This can either be a legitimate organizational structure demand, or it can just be the person being controlling due to their own insecurity. And in that case, this rule is also hard to justify. Finally, what are our key takeaways here? The first is that everyone has rules in every conflict caused by a breach of one of those rules.

The person may have that rule in an explicit or subconscious manner, but the violation is the same regardless of the case. The second is that it's crucial to clarify rules, regardless of whether the person explicitly knows the rule or not. They must communicate it to the other person, otherwise they can't avoid the other person. Breaking it again in the future. Rules can be reasonable or not. Some may be completely understandable, such as refusing to continue an argument when someone becomes emotional or aggressive, but others can be unfair and not tolerated. And finally, the goal of analyzing someone's rules is always to find a way to not break them later on to avoid subsequent conflicts.

And remember that you can find all key takeaways on the key takeaways wiki page. Both the link and the password are in the Book description for convenience so that you can just copy and paste them. So as we see when you have a conflict, it's probably because you broke or disrespected somebody's rule and it's very important for you to know what it is so that you can stop breaking it in the future, at least if it's a reasonable one.

Rule Analysis and Adaptation in Financial Services

There are multiple reasons why a conflict may have occurred, and it's always important to get to the bottom of it. People can become offended by varied reasons and why in some cases it may just be a personality thing or the person has a bad day. Usually there are specific reasons that you can identify. For example, the other side may have felt disrespected. For example, you get them off in a meeting, you insult their planning or models or evaluations or you disagree with them in front of investors or executives or any other action that could be perceived as disrespectful. It may also be that the other side feels treated unfairly. For example, they got passed up for promotion or they didn't get a compensation adjustment and so on.

If you're involved, this will be even worse. For example, if the person didn't get promoted, that's enough to make them have a hostile attitude. But if you're an analyst in the same team and they didn't get it, but you got it and they think that they deserve it more, they will be even more hostile towards you. So whatever the reason is, it's important that after fixing this conflict, naturally you go back and identify the root of the conflict and the rule that was broken so that you can avoid future ones because you don't break that rule in the future. So if they were offended because you cut them off, just don't cut them off in the future. This is naturally assuming that the rule is reasonable.

Techniques Intro

Let's talk about the techniques. That is if you've properly diagnosed a conflict. Now it's time to actually solve it. And there are a couple of communication tricks that we can use to focus the person on a solution to decrease the intensity of their emotions and a lot more. Let's cover this group of topics. If you've properly assessed the conflict that you have on your hands now, it's time to actually solve it. Using a myriad of techniques and tools. The different techniques that will cover all have elements in common, namely showing empathy and understanding for the other side's problem in order to more effectively disarm them, deactivating their emotions, to bring them back to the domain of logic and focusing on finding a solution, among other things. In order to achieve this, we are going to cover five different types of techniques. The first is respect and understanding, showing that you understand the other side's point of view in order to decrease their intensity.

Then comes comforting and supporting, letting someone lash out when they are in an emotional state while you persist to try and get across to them. After that, mediation and diplomacy, how do properly mediate a conflict between two other parties without being biased? After that come personal rules and boundaries. This is enforcing a rule and not tolerating something. Sometimes it starts small conflicts, but it also helps prevent bigger ones later. And finally, focusing on implementation, making a person focus on the solution for a problem and not the problem itself, but using specific wording to force them to do it. So as you see in this group of topics, we are going to focus on some techniques to get the person to drop their guard, to focus on a solution and a lot more.

Respect and Understanding

Let's talk about respect and understanding. Feeling disrespected is the source of many different conflicts. And even when it isn't someone feeling understood or feeling like you're on their side, or at least that you understand them is a great way to get them to drop their guard and be more reasonable. Let's take a look at how this works. If you think of concepts like empathy, connecting and understanding the other side, they are social skills in general, but they are especially important in de-escalating, tense situations. The core reason for this is that they decrease amygdala activation.

You can consider the amygdala your emotional brain, and it especially activates when you don't trust the other person when you're emotional, such as angry, disliking them, or any other intense negative situation. Empathy and respect help decrease this amygdala activation, bringing the person back to the domain of logic. But another reason for this is that respect and understanding make people accept something more easily. If you're trying to get the person to make a concession to settle for something or just accept something, this will work better if you show that you understand them first because they identify with you more so you have more power. There are three techniques that work especially well to show respect and understanding for the person.

These are, first of all, demonstrating empathy, taking what you think that the other side is feeling or thinking and verbalizing it back to them, saying things like, I know you must feel stressed or I know you must be frustrated with this, or even I know this is awkward. This helps calm the person down because they feel understood. The second is to tailor communication for the person's impulse archetypes. There are four different archetypes that correspond to whether the person focuses on the big picture versus the details and logic versus emotion.

For example, if they're focused on the big picture and they're logical, they are dominant. If they're focused on the details and they're logical, they are an analyst. Each type has specific language patterns that better persuade them.

So, for example, if they're dominant, they don't want to waste time and they want to know how they win. If you use their language, you can calm them down more easily. And finally, actually verbalizing respect for the person. This seems like a very small and specific technique, but it works so well, especially if the person's influence archetype is dominant. This will be an actual requirement of communicating with them. But in general, especially for people that have an ego or that are sensitive, it's always good to verbalize respect for them and it doesn't need to be something very sophisticated. Just saying something like, I know your time is valuable, so thank you for being here or I respect your authority and credentials.

You want to understand and respect the person's achievements. One side note you don't need to bring yourself down. You just need to raise them up. Specifically, one of the most frequent profiles that you will find are alpha or dominant people. This governance. There are specific techniques to deal with this type of personality, which you will find in any of my Books that include the desc, personality types or other resources. But these become important when you have a person that is on edge. And these can include first asking for the person's opinion. Dominant people hate to be excluded from things, and they love when others ask for their opinion and expertise. So even if you're not going to actually do anything with their opinion, just ask for it.

Ask them to validate something or to say what their thoughts are. This helps disarm them. The second is showing them how they can win and what they win from Exclusive. This is all that dominant. People care about being better than others. Show them how you can fix the situation and give them something that makes them win. Also verbalize respect. We just mentioned this. Show them that you respect their experience, credentials, authority and status. And finally, you'll have to make concessions. This is not as much of a technique as it is a necessity. A dominant is your worst negotiation nightmare because they will demand everything and give nothing whatever you're trying to accomplish.

Expect them to take a lot more than that and give you nothing in return. Dominance in specific are children who throw tantrums and. Town hall negotiations, if even a little detail of what they want is not respected, you will need to be the adult that takes the hits, gives them what they want and safeguards the negotiation. One last consideration when showing respect is that tense. People can be triggered by a lack of respect, not just for them individually, but others as well. Especially if the first party that you're disrespecting is someone close to them or if they have a heightened sense of justice. I have to confess that I myself am this way.

If I'm in a negotiation with you and I see you can align or not hold the door for somebody else that is completely unrelated to us, we're done here and many people are this way. They require you to be decent in general, and it's fun that the biggest example of this actually happens in the context of job interviews. The person is on the way to the building and they could argue or push somebody in the lobby entrance and they don't apologize for it. And then later they found out that it was the interviewer or someone related, and they're done. So remember to do things such as waiting in queues without cutting, using manners like please and thank you for holding doors for others, especially in yea or inside your office building, because you never know who that random person may be to do your research before suggesting things, showing respect and to be cautious, especially with people that think you are quote unquote below you like juniors, assistants, cleaning staff and others.

This happens both with situations in the real world or just in work. If you don't treat your own people well within the company, how are you going to treat a client? Well, which is true or not, is a very fair question. What are some implementation pointers? The first is to treat everyone as equals. One of the best ways to show respect is to show it to everyone. People that you pass by on the street, service workers, people with different status in the company. Let people see you as respectful under every circumstance, be graceful, Being respectful and keeping the quorum when others do so as well is easy. Being graceful when you're being attacked, though not so much. Don't take the bait when others are being less than graceful. Don't just turn it on. Being respectful should be a core tenet in life.

Don't do it just when you're in work mode or with important people, make sure that it's a personal trait regardless of the circumstances that you're in. And finally, hold yourself back. Remember inhibiting yourself when others are trying you and baiting you into stooping down to their level. Make sure that you don't, because that's a situation where you won't ever win. What are some do's and don'ts in terms of respect and understanding do's do either without fake? There is no such thing as too much respect. I mean, there is, but it's probably a lot more than what you think it is. Make sure to actively show that you're being respectful and considerate so that you don't give the other side a reason to attack.

You don't don't take it out on people, even people that you may consider that have no status or are below you probably are not. They just appear to be. And even when they are below you, well, you never know where you will be tomorrow or then. Don't give anyone a reason to hold a grudge in the future. What are some examples of showing respect and understanding? The first is just verbalizing. I know this is hard. Someone verbalizes to another person that they know how hard the situation is, but then unfortunately this change is still necessary. Cushions the blow to them. The second is verbalizing disagreement, saying something like I know you don't agree with this and I know you had your own plans, but unfortunately we will be doing this for example.

It also helps empathize and soften the blow in. Finally, another example is paying attention to the little things. These go a long way in showing respect for someone holding the door for them, not interrupting them, and so on. What are our key takeaways here? The first is using empathy. Take what you think the other side is feeling and simply verbalize it. I know you must be upset. I know that you must think that I'm not being reasonable. I know you must think that this is unfair and so on. You don't have to agree with it. You just have to verbalize it. Then understanding showing that you understand them goes a long way. Don't just force your decision on them. First, show that you understand their point of view and then say. This is necessary despite it. And finally, show respect. Many people underestimate the role of respect.

You don't need to kiss up, but you do need to make sure that you cover the basics so that the other side is not feeling disrespected. And remember that you can find all key takeaways on the key takeaways Wiki page. Both the link and the password are in the Book description for convenience so that you can just copy and paste them. So as we see respect, empathy and understanding are very important weapons. Although they seem like soft skills or intangible skills, they're very important to get the person to see you as an equal or to drop their guard, which makes resolving the conflict a lot easier later on.

Respect and Understanding in Financial Services

You can use the techniques mentioned to show respect and understanding of the other person that you have a conflict with, regardless of the specific financial service or their position within the company, you can leverage empathy by using simple statements such as I understand that you were expecting a promotion or I understand that you wanted a different fee structure, or even I understand that this is awkward or I understand that you have different expectations among others. Remember, you don't have to necessarily agree with the person. You just have to show understanding of their point of view. You can also tailor communication to their specific areas archetype. If they were dominant, they only care about not wasting time and winning, usually in the form of returns. So what was on those? If they are an analyst, they care about the system. The approval numbers, facts, figures focus on those.

If they are passionate, they care about the big vision, celebrating, partying, being an inspiration to others. Focus on that. And finally, if they are not sure they want to feel supportive, they want you to hold their hand and they want to know that you value the relationship. So that's what you focus on. And finally, you can also verbalize respect, especially for egotistical or sensitive people. So crucial you want to use statements such as, I value your time, I value your achievements. I am not going to ignore your importance or the effort that you make and so on. Remember, you don't have to put yourself down. You just have to bring them up.

Comforting and Supporting

Let's talk about comforting and supporting someone. When a person is in a heightened emotional state, they can be vicious and they can rush out in a very big way. So there are some techniques that we can use here to make the person come back down to logic, or even in minor situations when the person is uncomfortable. For example, there are still things that you can do to make them more comfortable. Let's take a look. Knowing how to properly support and comfort others is important. There will be two main types of situations where this skill is needed. First is comforting someone in terms of minor situations.

This happens very frequently and often we're talking about whether someone is uncomfortable and you choose the conversation topic that makes them the most comfortable to start a conversation when someone is bored to keep them company after they hear an unpleasant comment or to suggest a change when they're actually physically uncomfortable sitting in a weird position. Then you have the major situations when someone has been humiliated in public when they were told they're not getting that promotion, they have a serious personal or workplace issue or others being able to make them feel safe and support them properly in terms of severe situations.

There is one thing that this has in common with aggressive people, which is that they will have high amygdala activation or in other words, they're very emotional. The only difference is that when people are feeling unsafe or mourning for something, usually they take the avoidance route instead of the aggressive route. But in fact they can also take this one as well, which further complicates things for somebody trying to help them. So all techniques that you use should help them lower their amygdala activation here. Some of them are in common with conflict resolution, like showing respect and empathy, which can work. But for these cases in specific, there are usually two main techniques.

The first is to label their emotions, saying something like, I know you must be feeling stressed or I know you must feel sad due to this, or waving emotions helps the person make them logical and reduces the intensity of the actual emotion. It's a great tactic to use. You help decrease the intensity of that emotion by acknowledging it and then they become more reasonable after that. It increases trust by the person. What I mean by this is when the person trusts you, they feel safer. Therefore, the best person to help someone feel comfortable or safe is the person that they trust the most.

And this also means that whatever you can do to increase trust and connection with the person will make your words have more weight and they will let you disarm their emotions more easily. Also important to mention is the fact that in the recovery process, some people can lash out and especially if they are close to you, they may lash out at you in specific and blame you in a personal way. This doesn't mean that you did anything wrong. It's just the person displacing their emotional outburst. But it sure feels personal. So when supporting and comforting others, one of the keys is to be able to take the hits, to take a few bites and understand that this is not personal. Just as we discussed in conflict, they are usually going to take one of two stances: hot or cold conflicts.

Either they are completely shut down, become cold, avoid reality altogether, or they are going to become too violent, aggressive or even abusive. And you need to be able to deal with both in more detail. They can do things such as, number one, just avoiding the issue, running away from it at full speed and not wanting to face it, or even becoming delusional and not seeing reality. Also, they can simply go cold. They can feel a lot of emotions and have opinions on the issue, but simply not reveal them. They switch their emotions off so that they don't feel the pain of the situation. A third option is fake agreement. They can pretend to agree with you and just lie to your face to get it out of the way and go back to self pity.

Or they may have some future plans, including possible revenge that they're not sharing with you. And finally, we have good old aggression, blaming you, insulting you, shirking responsibility and shifting it on you, among other possibilities. What are some implementation pointers in terms of comforting and supporting? First, the focus is to help the person regain function. The biggest goal when someone is in crisis mode is to help them become functional again. It's not just about removing emotion, it's about removing emotion and clearing the way for them. To be able to function again. Coping mechanisms are key here in crisis management.

Also, solving a crisis is precisely about making sure that this person has good enough coping mechanisms to help them keep their mental health. What I mean is that they're all coping mechanisms may not be enough to deal with this new issue. Of course, it's a sensitive issue to ask how a colleague is going to deal with something, but do it. Try and ask what coping mechanisms they do have, whether they are enough and even suggest some new ones. Gestures may work. Some people feel supported by conversation and the helping hand, but other people can feel supported by a gift, even if symbolic, either a personal one or by their team or a group of friends. Finally, be fair. If people see you comforting a colleague, but not another one when they are in similar situations, they all know that you are being partial and that is a massive red flag.

What are some do's and don'ts in terms of comforting and supporting someone? Don't focus on safety. This means don't let the person feel judged or attacked. Be as open as possible to facilitate their recovery.

One sniff of a judgmental attitude and the person can retreat right back to the bottom. Don'ts. Don't rush it. Nobody has a recovery schedule. Some people can bounce back quickly, but others may take time. Trying to rush someone into recovering in a specific timeline can backfire and make it worse. What are some examples of comforting and supporting? The first example is absorbing someone's aggression. Maybe you give someone some very bad news, such as them being fired and they take it out on you.

Stay objective and weather the hits. They're just lashing out until they calm down. The second example is absorbing grief. Maybe someone lost someone or something important and you need to comfort them until they get back up on their feet. And finally, another example is bridging avoidance. When someone is withdrawing, you need to keep politely insisting or maybe give them some time and then circle back, always supporting them until they recover. What are our key takeaways here? The first is that just like with conflict itself, there are multiple reactions that people may have when they need support. Also hot and cold and very similar to the types that we've already covered. In order to comfort them, you must persist. The second is that using labeling and increasing trust does help.

All emotion comes from the amygdala. So any technique that decreases amygdala activation brings people back to the realm of logic. Labeling their emotions and obtaining more trust from them are just two examples. And finally, expect to take a few hits. When you're trying to comfort someone who has very intense emotions, it's possible that they will lash out at you. It's not personal. It's just collateral damage. And you have to go through this in order to help them recover.

And remember that you can find all key takeaways on the key takeaways Wiki page. Both the link and the password are in the Book description for convenience so that you can just copy and paste them. So as we see, especially in emotional situations, you are going to take a few hits while the person transitions from emotion to logic in the right to techniques that we can use here. Either the person that they trust the most can speak with them, or you can actively use affect labeling to make the person's emotions decrease in intensity.

Comforting and Supporting in Financial Services

When a colleague or friend, manager, PM or any other co-worker in financial services is emotional, it's important to know whether the hits, as they slowly calm down and accept the hit that they took in there, will be hits. Some people can lash out in a very vicious way when they're emotional. There are two techniques here that we can leverage, as mentioned. The first is the leverage, the existing level of trust, the person that this person trusts the most to help calm them down. The more that you trust someone, the more that person is able to help deactivate their amygdala in their emotions.

But also you can magnify the trust you already have if you actively remind the person of situations when this person was a trusted advisor, an objective third party that had their best interests in mind, they are going to trust them even more and its effect is amplified. Also, you can on average affect labeling using statements such as you seem angry or you seem this appointment will all help diffuse the person's emotions, because when you label an emotion, it loses intensity and it helps make them come back to logic faster.

Mediation and Diplomacy

Let's talk about mediation and diplomacy. That is, there are situations where you are not involved in a conflict, but you are judging an external conflict and you have to see the merit in both sides. And sometimes you have to render an opinion impartially and objective. So how do you do that? It's not necessarily easier than being in a conflict yourself. So let's take a look at how this works. The capacity to mediate conflicts between other people and remaining partial in the face of them is crucial. You need to be able to effectively detach the logical facts from the personal opinions of the different parties and then help them come to an equitable resolution for everyone.

Mediating a conflict between other people is not that much easier than being involved in one yourself. The same techniques and dynamics from conflicts where you actually are One of the involved parties also apply here, as do some techniques like internalizing removing yourself from the personal side of things, as well as discussing from first principles, separating the facts from the opinions. One of the most important topics when mediating conflicts, among others, is to realize which rules were broken. As we saw, conflict is always a consequence of someone breaking a rule. A person may have offended another person by interrupting them, not listening to them, stereotyping them in a myriad other possible causes.

It's important to know which rules were broken so that you can both diagnose the cause of the conflict, but also prevent it from occurring again. Restoring trust between both parties and allowing them to work together in the future. You need to ask yourself and ask the conflicting parties as well, which attitude may have happened that actually triggered the conflict? Was it a disagreement? Was it someone ignoring the other person, someone patronizing the other person? Was it mutual? And how serious was it? And then figure out how to crystalize those rules formally. For example, John feels offended if someone cuts him off while he's speaking, and it's important to do it with both parties this way.

They know exactly what they have to avoid so that they don't accidentally or purposefully trigger the other person. And then ask yourself and ask the people involved whether they are willing to work together or be together again afterwards. Is there common ground among them? Does each side commit to honoring the other side's rules or not at all? What are some pointers when mediating conflicts? First, find the trigger. There's usually one key occurrence that triggers the conflict, or maybe a medium one, followed by a serious one that actually compounded and escalated the original situation. But the point is to find out what triggered each side and specifically align with the company culture.

The one side caused a conflict because they went against an expected company culture behavior or on the other hand, were they actually following the expected processes and it was the other side who took it personally? Make both sides verbalize respect. This is key. If people don't respect each other and they are not willing to put effort into solving this or even if they are, but they refuse to speak verbally to each other, maybe none of them should be in the team and finally make the rules clear. All of us know that some things trigger us, but maybe we don't know exactly what they are. It's important to do the work, to dig deep and clarify what specific rules were broken for each side.

What are some do's and don'ts when mediating conflicts do you where you can project on people here as well? There may be cases where you're meditating and you like a person or you believe a person more than the other. And it takes a large amount of effort and willpower to remain objective instead of going with your biases here. So be aware of this.

Don't take it lightly. Conflicts are many times deeply personal. If the person thinks that you're just trying to make this better and hurry up to get it out of the way, paying lip service to it, but not actually doing anything, they won't be honest and the conflict won't really be gone. Unfortunately, this is what HR does in many companies in the world.

What are some examples of mediation and diplomacy? The first is a simple argument between people. You're in the middle and they ask you to meditate. Maybe it's two friends having a tiff, maybe it's two colleagues arguing over proposals, but this can go very wrong very quickly. The best way is to be objective, stating the merit of both people and calming them both down. Then a similar example is a workplace conflict. Two coworkers are butting heads over their proposals for something at work. Verbalize the. Merit of both in the respect that you have for both and pick the best one. Objectively. The first and final example is intense aggression.

If you're between two people that just hate each other's guts and things are escalating, you need to empathize with both again, being objective and bringing them to the realm of logic, deactivating their emotions, and after that, objectively deciding from first principles based on facts only. What are our key takeaways here? The first is to start from first principles, or in other words, facts and not opinions. Reduce both people's opinions to the core facts. And aside from those facts, only the second is being impartial. It's crucial that you don't show any preference for any of the people involved, objectively state the facts and treat both people with the same level of respect and finally look for compliance.

Our goal here, after analyzing rules and determining a good outcome, is to know how we can prevent this in the future. And if both people aren't willing to work together or to be together after this, there's really no point. And remember that you can find all key takeaways on the key takeaways Wiki page. Both the link and the password are in the Book description for convenience so that you can just copy and paste them. So as we see when mediating a conflict between two parties, it's crucial to start from first principles. That is, start from logic, start from the facts and nothing else, but also look for compliance. That is, even if the two parties say that they're going to work together and that everything is fine, what steps are they actually going to take to solve this issue?

Mediation and Diplomacy in Financial Services

In many different situations, you'll find yourself mediating conflicts between coworkers, be that the junior, senior or even partner level or even between co-workers and the company or between a co-worker and the client or investor, for example, in these cases always keep in mind the following guidelines. First of all, always act as an objective third party, a trusted advisor, make sure that people stick to the facts and not opinions. In fact, check them on what they say. Don't let them get away with creative facts or alternative facts or interpretations.

You want to play the role of the trusted advisor that sees the merit in every side, but that also holds every side accountable. Second, making sure that everyone feels heard, especially if there are sensitive people involved or people with a big ego not being heard is the first step to escalating a conflict. So make sure that it doesn't happen. And finally, make sure to leave all parties to an equitable conclusion that leaves everyone as satisfied as possible or more likely is a little and satisfied as possible.

Personal Rules/Boundaries

Let's talk about personal rules and boundaries. This may sound counterintuitive, but one of the best ways to solve conflicts is to know which conflicts you don't even want to let begin in the first place. There are some things that you should just not tolerate, and drawing boundaries has some specific nuances to it. So let's take a look at how to use this technique. Personal boundaries are key to effective conflict resolution, or more specifically, they help create small conflicts to avoid bigger ones later. As we know, every conflict derives from a break in somebody rules in personal boundaries are how you actually enforce those rules.

It's when someone does something that you just don't tolerate you letting them know to their face right then and there, but in a polite way. For example, if someone asks you to take care of something that might not be your responsibility, you can reply with something such as Unfortunately, I don't have the ability to do this right now. Or when someone asks you to take notes in a meeting, for example, and that is not your responsibility, you can reply with, I'm sorry, but I'm not in a position to take care of this right now. Or when someone asks you to work on the weekend, you simply say, Unfortunately I can. You may have these rules about what you tolerate or not, but actually enforcing them comes down to personal boundaries, what you accept or not from the people around you.

Although this may seem uncomfortable at first, especially for people that are not used to doing it, very shy, very permissive, because this creates smaller conflicts in the present. They are, however, essential for you to stand up for yourself and not bottle things up. Doing the latter will only create a bigger conflict down the road. So by drawing boundaries, you're kind of front loading the conflict. You're willing to have a smaller issue now instead of letting it drag on and become a very big one later. In terms of corporate behaviors in specific boundaries are also crucial to stop and acceptable behaviors in their tracks from the beginning.

Because if you don't draw a boundary the first time or the second time that someone does something incorrect, they will just keep doing it. If someone speaks over you or cuts you off at a meeting, or you're a woman and they call you honey or act condescending and you actually tolerate it instead of immediately drawing the boundary. And if this keeps going for multiple times, they will become used to it and just keep doing it. So boundaries are crucial to send a message that the person cannot get away with this because otherwise they believe that they can do anything without consequence because they can.

At the core of personal boundaries is the mindset that people have to know that you're not a pushover. You have your limit and people can't cross you. It can be a big limit. You can have a lot of patience, but people have to know that it will run out if they cross you. If they try to abuse you, they are going to get a reaction because otherwise you're just a pushover and they can just do whatever they want. Personal boundaries are how you show this. In some cultures, it's known as the concept of showing teeth just like an animal. You have limits that if crossed, they are going to cause a proportionate or even disproportionate reaction.

And this inhibits people from abusing you. The key here is that you don't have to draw boundaries on everything. You just seem very irritating and hard to get along with. But you do need to show this for one or two key areas. People have to know that there is a limit somewhere that they can cross. What are some implementation pointers for personal boundaries? The first is to be reasonable. Some people have too many rules and boundaries to the point of being ridiculous. Don't ask me things before 10 a.m.. Don't talk about topics that I'm not comfortable with in front of me and many of the rules.

So be reasonable. Another one is to make it a point to respect other people's boundaries, because boundaries are not just for you but others. The best way to have others respect your rules is to respect theirs as well. If you don't want to be bothered during lunch time and a person that doesn't like to be bothered during the afternoon, then you know what you should do in order for them to respect your rule. Another point is equality. Boundaries are only effective if you draw them with everyone, and that's the beauty of it. It should be an automatic reaction. People must get the impression that this is a part of your personality, that it doesn't change depending on the person. If it does, it loses its effect.

And finally, you can draw boundaries on things both big and small. You can draw the boundary on a very big request from your manager to work overtime for multiple weeks or just on people chatting near you at a very high volume when you're trying to concentrate. The mechanism is exactly the same. What are some dos and don'ts in terms of personal boundaries? Do so like the boundaries that are the most important to you. Don't start fights just to prove a point. Defend what really matters to you. Don'ts. Don't be too exaggerated in your response. You don't want to break a relationship or kind of push an ultimatum. You just want to show the person that you don't accept this, but then continue the relationship as is with nothing changed.

It's just that I don't accept this and everything's fine. What are some examples of personal rules and boundaries? The first is someone refusing to work over time. Their manager is trying to pressure them into working overtime and they simply politely reply, I'm sorry, but I can't do it. This is an example. Another is politely disagreeing with the manager. They may give you directions to follow blindly without questioning and you politely say, I disagree with this approach unless you give me a justification. And finally refusing to be called certain names is another one. You may have a colleague that is just acting too familiar, calling you lazy or dumb as a comment, even if as a joke, but you politely tell them to their face that you will not tolerate this.

So what are our key takeaways here? The first is that personal boundaries are how you enforce your personal rules. You may have a rule of not tolerating a certain behavior, but only by drawing the boundary do you prevent someone from doing it. Boundaries are crucial to stop negative behaviors right away. Don't tolerate over time or offensive behavior the first time and the person will never ask a second one. And finally, boundaries can be drawn on multiple topics and for multiple attitudes only. You know what you tolerate from others. And remember that you can find all key takeaways on the key takeaways Wiki page. Both the link and the password are in the Book description for convenience so that you can just copy and paste them.

So as we see, you don't need to draw boundaries on every single thing. You should have your core rules and defend only the principles that you really stand for. But it's very important that when you don't tolerate the situation, don't even get into a conflict about that. Remove yourself from the situation from the beginning. And remember, don't let it become a habit. Don't let bad things become a habit. Whenever you see behavior that is not acceptable, draw the boundary right away because it's not going to get better with time.

Personal Rules/Boundaries in Financial Services

The best way to use personal boundaries in terms of conflicts with other co-workers or managers is to politely draw boundaries on the topics that you don't accept. Finance can be a brutal industry, and it's very easy to mix up rigid criticism and personal attacks, especially for aggressive or narcissistic readers. So you should tolerate the former. Absolutely. For example, a manager questioning your research model or your numbers, but never the latter. You can do this by using simple statements such as I'm sorry, but I don't tolerate this or I don't accept this, or even I am not in a position to deal with this right now. This will both help others shape their behavior to what you accept because they now know what you react to and what you block. But it also allows you to remove yourself from the conflicts that you don't want, because if you enforce a personal boundary, the conflict doesn't even begin.

Implementation Focus

Let's talk about implementation focus. This technique is very devious. It consists of leading the person into finding a solution for the problem themselves. So they think that they're the ones who came up with the idea You don't need to do any work at all, and they are going to solve the situation by themselves. It sounds magic, but it's a real technique. Let's take a look at how it works when dealing with conflicts. It's probably basic to say by this point that one should focus on the solution and not on the problem. Sure, analyze people's rules, figure out the root cause of why this happened, but it's better to not linger on the problem and to move on to the solution itself. In practical terms, the best way to actually make this happen is to use the psychological principle of implementation intention.

This is a principle that dictates that focusing on the how of doing something on the implementation convinces people to do it more easily. This principle was verified at first with a study where they wanted people to vote and they had two groups in one group. They just asked a person whether they would vote or not for the other one. They asked how they would vote. Which road will you take? What time of the day are you going? And so on. In short, they focused on the implementation of that idea and the latter convinced a lot more people to vote. This principle can actually be applied in any area of life to persuade people more easily.

For example, instead of asking Will you vote? How will you vote when selling? Instead of will you buy? How will you buy the same for conflicts? Instead of asking, will you get along with this person, asking How will you get along with this person? Or How can we make sure this doesn't happen again? And so on. In most cases, this can be achieved by simply using questions or statements that force the person to visualize the specifics of implementing this change. As we saw. These can include, for example, tell me how we can make this happen. Tell me how you will work together.

Tell me how we'll avoid this in the future and so on. Or what do I need to do in order for you to complete this or what needs to happen in order to get this done? Or, for example, how can we make sure this never happens again? Or even what would need to happen here for you to consider this a success? Or simply how can we make sure this doesn't happen or tell me what needs to happen so that this doesn't repeat itself or any other question or statement? Remember, you just have to force the person to focus on the implementation of the thing. The beauty of this technique is that not only will the person come up with a solution, but possibly they'll even think that it was their own idea in the first place.

This is a brilliant technique, putting it in layman's terms to get someone to collaborate with you when they don't want to. What are some implementation pointers for while implementing a plan that is not intended? The first is that implementation intention is a principle that can be leveraged for any topic. Just make the person visualize the implementation of anything and they will be more easily persuaded. Also, things are always solvable. Using this technique will make sure that the other side gives you a solution, although it may not be the solution that you want, they will always generate a solution. This principle can be used to unblock situations.

You can be proactive in asking how to get something done, but you can also use it as a response to a no to unblock options. For example, if someone tells you there is no way that we'll be able to work together, you can ask what would need to happen for you to work together. Finally, you can ask about any specifics. As long as you ask about the specifics, what attitude will you need to make this happen? What timeframe would you have in mind? What methods will you use? How can you make it happen? What needs to happen for you to accomplish this? And so on? What are some dos and don'ts with implementation? Do make use of this tool in different scenarios. You can always leverage it to get someone to collaborate with you.

Don'ts. Don't ask this in a hypothetical manner. Use this principle to ask about specifics to get things done. How will you get along with the person? How are we going to prevent this from happening again? And so on? Very practical. What are some examples of having an implementation focus? The first is for closing a deal. When you're trying to negotiate with someone and getting nowhere, asking them how can we make this happen? Can make the other side come up with a solution. Another example is working together when two people don't. Getting along that well, asking the other person how you can work together or what needs to happen for you to be able to work together can help them think of the specifics that may help the situation.

The fourth and final example is improving something. This technique can be used to overcome difficulties, but also to improve good things. Asking how we can make this even better may generate interesting solutions. What are our key takeaways here? The first is implementation. Intention, as the name says, is all about well implementing, forcing a person to think of how they will do something which makes them visualize it and come up with a solution and at the end of the day more easily do it. It can be used as a question or a statement. Any format works as long as at the end of the day you ask about the details of implementing this.

Remember, there's always a solution. This technique is very effective because it forces the person to come up with an answer. It may not be exactly the answer that you want, but there always is an answer. Finally, the magic of this technique is that it will make the person think that it was their own idea if they are the ones generating options. And remember that you can find all key takeaways on the key takeaways wiki page. Both the link and the password are in the Book description for convenience so that you can just copy and paste them. So as we see, implementation is kind of a form of augmented visualization, you want the person to focus on a solution and you want them to imagine the details with such specificity that you really see how they would do it, and then they're more likely to do it at the end of the day.

Implementation Focus in Financial Services

You can easily direct a person to a solution to a conflict by leveraging statements and questions that focus on the specifics of that solution. For example, what needs to happen for us to solve this conflict or tell me what needs to happen for you both to be able to work well together in the future? Or what can I do to make sure that you work well with this client in the future? Or what can I do to make sure that you collaborate with this analyst? Or how can we make sure this rule is not broken anymore? Or what needs to happen to make sure this relationship is safeguarded in the future? By using these, the other side is more likely to actually put a solution to work because they've already pictured that solution in their mind.

Introduction

Let's talk about the traps in this group of topics. We are going to cover the different possible traps that you may fall into which can make a conflict actually worse. And these are not necessarily exclusively related to the techniques. You can do all of the right things, but also be doing the wrong ones. So you need to actively avoid the traps. Let's go over some traps in this group of topics. Even if you have properly diagnosed the conflicts and you are using the techniques to effectively handle it. There are still some attitudes that you can take subconsciously that can make things worse and actually take away some of the progress made or even all of it.

In many cases, you may not even realize that you're taking these attitudes and they can have serious consequences for the relationship because they antagonize the other side. We are going to take a look at some of these traps that you can just fall into even when you don't realize it. In order for you to be aware of them and avoid them during your interaction for this, we are going to cover two main families of traps that you can fall into. The first are escalation traps. These are attitudes that make the other side angrier or feel this respective and that make the situation just worse.

Then we'll cover misalignment traps. These are traps that make the other side have different expectations than yours, either on purpose or through negligence by you, and that usually avoid a short term problem to create a much bigger one later. So as we see, there are many traps that you can fall into during a conflict and we are going to cover misalignment traps. That is when you're not thinking about the same thing as they are or escalation traps when you actively do something to make the situation worse.

Misalignment Traps

Let's talk about misalignment traps. These are traps when you're not thinking about the same thing as the other side. Maybe the expectations are different. Maybe you actually promise something that you can deliver or others. Sometimes we do this to get a hard conversation out of the way, or just because we're afraid of actually having that conversation. But as we're going to see, the situation doesn't get better. It just gets worse. So let's take a look at some types of misalignment traps. There are some cases where you may read a person or mislead a person to think something untrue, willingly or not. And in every single case, this will come back to bite you later, because just like any other problem, if it's ignored, it's going to grow and fester.

It may be something that you promised and that, you know, is just not going to come true or having agreed to something hastily just to close the topic. That is not exactly what you can deliver. But regardless, all of these decisions will come back to haunt you later. There are three main traps of this type that you should look out for here. The first is misaligned expectations. By this I mean you think that one thing will happen, but the person thinks that another thing will. Maybe it's a client that thinks that you're going to get a refund because others in the same situation have and you don't bother to correct them. Or your manager telling a subordinate that this type of work gets them promoted and now they're thinking that it will. But you know very well that it's not that simple.

The second type is hurrying an issue. When a situation is too awkward or tense, you simply agree to things that you otherwise wouldn't just to get it out of the way. For example, as a manager saying something like, Yes, I'm sure you'll get rewarded for the project later, just do it now and later they don't. Or a third type, which is you actually making a false promise. You tell someone to their face that they're going to get something that you know very well that they never will. The problem with all of these is that you're avoiding a current small problem in the present by kicking it down to the future, either to make someone accept something more easily or just to hurry up an issue and avoid attention.

But either way, you are causing a massive problem down the road. And as we saw for any type of problem, letting it grow will only make it worse because the person is going to pile on more and more expectations and assumptions based on what you said as time goes by. So when you wait to have the conflict later, it's going to hit much harder in terms of alignment and will only grow much bigger. The common issue behind this is that many times we say what we don't mean in order to kill the tension. For example, you're sitting with someone important, a client, a manager, a subordinate, and you know what you have to say. But sometimes you just don't have the courage to say no, especially when the other person has status or authority.

This is, for example, the subordinate that is asked to participate in a project that they know is going to be massive over time and that is going to do nothing for them. Under normal conditions, they would refuse. But in the heat of the moment, with the boss looking them in the face, they just say, Sure, and now you are in a prison of your own making. But therefore the solution is simple as well. It's to gently persist with your point, regardless of how tense or difficult the situation may be, you need to have that capability to look the person in the eyes, no matter how important, no matter how intense, and hold that tension in, not break it when the other person insists.

In short, especially with important people, you will have an immediate reflex of killing the tension when the other person insists will lose that reflex. Don't kill the tension. It's that simple. What are some implementation pointers in terms of avoiding these misalignment traps? The first is that the more difficult the situation, the more important that this actually is. When someone is trying to extract a big promise from you versus a small one, or when it's someone of authority versus someone that's an equal. The difficulty level will be much higher, but so is the potential for you losing a lot more. Therefore, the more difficult that things are, the more that you think that you can't do it, the more important it is for you not to give in.

Then this comes down to being honest, to not misleading others. But also even if you were not the one to do it, if the person is misleading themselves to still intervene and correct them despite how hard and awkward this conversation may be. This. Will involve some half truths. Being honest and adjusting someone's expectations may make them disappointed or angry, but the alternative is them becoming even angrier and more disappointed when this explodes. And finally, focus on corrections on every little detail. Even when people agree on the big picture, they may disagree on the details or the time frame or many other specificities.

Try to uncover what they think. Incorrect them when they're not being reasonable. What are some dos and don'ts in terms of misalignment? Do make it a point to always check with the person whether they understand and agree with something. Make this a constant practice so that you never have an unpleasant surprise. Don'ts. Don't think that the other person is fully responsible for what they think. Because if they have the wrong expectation and you know this and you didn't correct them, you're just as guilty. What are some examples of traps that cause misalignment? The first is someone getting fired.

When the manager is trying to negotiate the terms, they're too nice and they end up promising things that they can't deliver on, such as that they'll pay their full salary or something similar for a couple of months and then they can't. And this type of situation always blows up.

Another one is Heretics in a company. What I mean is when someone disbelieves their manager and openly confronts them on everything, casting doubt and poisoning others, if the manager doesn't tell them the truth, which is that they have to go now, but instead of lies or sugarcoat it, telling them that they can stay just to kill the tension, this usually ends up becoming very ugly. And finally, promises made to friends are another example.

It may be the case that a friend is going down and you promise them something to go out with them or similar activity when you know full well that you're not going to do it later. And then this becomes even much more of a letdown. What are our key takeaways here? The first is that there are always three main ways to spark misalignment. Having different expectations, hiring the issue, or actively promising false things. Remember, this will always come back to bite you later. People will take your words seriously and they will draw conclusions and assumptions based on. So you're avoiding a small problem now that is going to become much bigger later on.

Misleading can take many forms. Active and passive. You can actively lead someone to believe something different from reality or simply not correct them when they do believe it themselves. But it's the same thing at the end of the day. And remember that you can find all key takeaways on the key takeaways wiki page. Both the link and the password are in the Book description for convenience so that you can just copy and paste them. So as we see, it's crucial to prevent any type of misalignment, whether you are actively leading someone on or they just got the wrong expectations on their own, you always have to see this is your responsibility. If you don't align those expectations, the problem is not going to go away, or it may go away, but it's going to come back later ten times as big. So you always have to fix this.

Misalignment Traps in Financial Services

You could avoid most misalignment traps with coworkers, investors, financial advisers and others by not making false promises or deceiving them in the first place, but also by immediately addressing them when they have different expectations. So if your client assumes that they are going to have a reduced management fee for their assets a year from now, and you know that it's going to stay the same, address that right away. Don't let them keep that illusion, that wrong expectation or this is going to backfire later. Or if a co-worker who is an analyst expects to not need to generate investment ideas every week. But you actually know this is necessary and that not doing it will actually cause problems for the fund. Addressed it right away. Don't let the person for themselves. In short, you don't want to give the other side any reason they have the wrong expectations. And even if they do anyway, you want to make sure to correct them right away.

Escalation Traps

Let's talk about escalation traps. There are things that you can do which make a situation even worse, not giving the person your full attention or making it seem like their problem is too easy to fix or otherwise not respecting them. The problem with escalation traps is that they're very easy to fall into without even realizing it. So let's cover some of these types among all the different attitudes that you can take in a tense situation. There are some that are sure to escalate the situation further, and naturally these should be avoided at all costs if you're looking to mediate or to resolve a conflict, because honestly, they will just make things worse, possibly much worse.

In specific, you should look out for these three, although they're kind of related to each other and can be considered variations of just not caring. They are specific manifestations. The first is being patronizing and or not taking the person seriously. Even when you can't do anything to actually help the person. Never make it seem like this is easy or that it can be solved easily because that would just make the person feel disrespected and decrease identification and trust. The second one is showing off or acting superior. It's related to the previous one. This hurts empathy and comes across as disrespectful because the person feels like you're not being honest or you just don't care.

And finally, actually not caring or lacking attention, simply not taking care of something or not doing it in time or not doing something. When you say you are going to do it, arriving late, among other things, this is the opposite of using a personal touch where the person knows that you're really putting in a lot more effort than you should here. They know that you're putting in less effort than you should, although these patterns are somewhat specific, your general goal should be to never give the impression that you're too comfortable or that this is too easy because that underestimates the person. It makes it seem like they're too little or too easy to deal with, or that the problem is not worth your time. And that is a recipe for disaster.

When this happens, the person will be angered because in a way they want to see you suffer or not necessarily suffer, but they want to see you vulnerable, genuine, with no shields, no excuses, no BS. They want to see that you take this conflict seriously. And when you don't, when you don't worry or you're not stressed, the person will just assume that you don't care whether this is true or not. So a technique that actually works well here is even mirroring their mood when they're stressed. You can see stress as well. When they're worried, you can seem worried as well. If they're angry at your company apartment that caused an issue, seem angry at them as well, even if you aren't just mirroring their mood, it makes the person assume that you're taking this more seriously.

What are some implementation pointers in terms of avoiding escalation traps? First, share the pain. Mirroring and verbalizing their feelings. Helps you show that you're understanding of their pain, you're involved in it and just this goes a long way. Use similar stories. We've all felt similar anger, indignities or other negative reactions to certain situations. So verbalizing a story where you yourself felt something similar to them helps establish commonalities and empathy. Then be honest. More than anything, hiding things or not being honest is going to trigger the person and break trust. Don't defend, don't deflect. Just be honest about what is wrong. Establish common ground if possible.

Commonalities help the other side identify with you in all. Empathy and understanding will be accelerated. Besides feeling like them, you are also actually like them. They will be even easier to persuade. What are some do's and don'ts when avoiding these escalation traps? Do put effort and attention into it. Besides showing that you care, putting in effort is the best technique at its core. The other side just wants to know that you're putting in the due effort and honoring the process. Even if you can't obtain immediate results or a solution, at least show that you're trying to don'ts. Don't do anything that makes you relate less to the person Being patronizing.

Not caring and being distracted are just examples, but they're not the whole range of attitudes by any means. So in general, avoid anything like that. It'll just send a signal to the person that you don't care. What are some examples of escalation traps? The first is not giving someone updates. For example, when you're fixing an urgent issue and you promise to give the client some frequent reports, maybe every 2 hours every day and you just don't. Or possibly even worse, you do have an update to send them with good information, but you just don't communicate it. This will just make people angry. Another example is false promises. When you promise to do something, but you don't, the person will believe that you think that they're not worth your time anyway, or that they don't deserve your best effort.

So be honest about what you can do from the start, because otherwise you're just setting them up for disappointment and finally, not matching their mood can also be a serious issue if they are angry or sad. They want you to feel the same way. In a sense, if you're happy and nonchalant, they will think that you don't care even if you do. What are our key takeaways here? The first, remember, is showing effort, not escalating. A situation in many cases comes down to showing that you're doing everything that you can, showing that you are constantly trying to fix this and that the person has your full attention. The moment that they think they don't have your attention, that's when they start to get angry and to escalate the situation. The second is to read yourself suffering from osmosis a little bit.

In many cases, when the other side is suffering in terms of something, they want you to suffer as well. So even if you don't have their pain, at least feel their pain. Show them that you are and finally take it seriously. Even if you can't do anything more to help the person or you just can't put more time into it. At least have the attitude that you wanted to that you would have if you could have that you are at least putting in all the effort and dedication that you can and remember that you can find all key takeaways on the key takeaways Wiki page.

Both the link and the password are in the Book description for convenience so that you can just copy and paste them. So as we see avoiding escalation traps at the end of the day comes down to showing that you are taking this seriously to the other side. You are not underestimating them, you value their time. You are suffering due to this weather a lot or not at all. But at the end of the day you are not underestimating them and you are not disrespecting them.

Escalation Traps in Financial Services

You can avoid escalating the conflict with a co-worker, a partner or a client in any type of financial service by keeping some things in mind, first of all, you want to feel their pain. So even if you don't agree with their position, make sure to at least show that you understand it. Listen closely, not merely their words, make them feel understood after that, and communicate constantly. Chances are a bitter conflict will not be solved overnight. It's about constantly interacting and slowly showing trust in doing more and more as the relationship improves. And finally, don't make it seem easy when the other side shares important points. If you take it lightly and you seem too carefree or too happy that you seem disrespectful, you want to almost show that you're suffering with them. Don't make this problem seem small in comparison to other things. That's what it seems when you're too happy overall.

Recap

We are now at the end of the conflict resolution Book. Let's take a moment to cover all of the different chapters and the topics that we've covered throughout this Book. With this, we close the conflict resolution chapter. Our goal here was to learn how to properly de-escalate and resolve tense situations with others in order to achieve a common goal. For this purpose, we covered three main families of topics. The first was the diagnostic being able to properly assess what type of conflict you're dealing with, as well as what may have caused it. Then the techniques themselves cover the different techniques that you can use to resolve conflicts such as empathy, comforting and supporting, showing respect, personal boundaries and others.

And finally, the traps, the telling, the most common traps that you must avoid in order to productively resolve these conflicts. What are some questions that you can ask yourself to consolidate the knowledge in this chapter? Am I properly empathizing with and showing respect for others, or am I possibly falling into traps that I'm not even aware of? Do I remain grounded to the facts and to first principles while mediating other conflicts in my impartial? Am I making false promises or at least not correcting others when they have different expectations of me themselves? Am I both making use of my personal boundaries and respecting other peoples? And am I making others focus on implementation or am I dwelling on a problem? Our plan of attack for this chapter should be the following.

First, making an accurate diagnosis. In short, what type of conflict do you have on your hands and what caused it in the first place? Then, using the tools that we mentioned to actually resolve the conflict, empathy, respect, implementation, focus, comforting and supporting and so on. And finally, always keeping in mind the possible traps and avoiding falling into them. Don't make things seem too easy or disrespect the person or give the impression that you have better things to do. Do have the hard conversations to align expectations and so on. With this, we close the conflict resolution chapter. Our goal in this chapter was to effectively solve and de-escalate tense situations. With this, we conclude the conflict resolution Book. I hope that this Book has given you actionable weapons and knowledge to solve or at least de-escalate the conflicts in your life. Thank you so much for reading.

Exclusion Confirmation

Let's talk about exclusion, confirmation. This is a technique that you may know and you may have used yourself, maybe not by this name, but it's what people refer to as reverse psychology. It's when you tell someone, you know what, this may not be for you and you gauge whether the person chooses or not, possibly excluding the other person serves as an excuse for them to back out. But it also creates intrigue and interest. You can easily achieve it by saying something like this may not be for you or this may not be for everyone. But I do have this if you're interested and want to take a look.

And naturally, not everyone here will chase some people or actually say, you know what, this isn't for me, but it doesn't mean that's the end. It just means they have an objection and now you can deal with it. The technique itself works even better if you qualify what you're offering. In short, you show them something that's exactly for them. And then you say this may not be for you. Of course it is saying it's in the format's. I don't know if this is for you, but I have a project or a product or service or a candidate or a value proposition. That is exactly what a wealthy or sophisticated person would like. But I don't know if it's for you. And the key is they have that exact trait.

It makes it seem like you're excluding something that is exactly for them. So they chase, for example, if you're positioning a project to a person, one of your employees, and you know that they're a high achiever and sophisticated, you could say something like, I don't know if this is for you, but I do have a project that's the type that only high achievers and sophisticated employees like. But I don't know if it would be for you. Tell me what you think. And Of course, they will want to be put in situations where you are more comfortable with the person and you have more trust with them. You can even use a variation, which is accusation almost in a playful manner, saying something such as, Oh, I'm sure that you won't even remember us.

We're just another supplier, right? You probably have three hundred on your list. We're saying, oh, I'm just another candidate in a sea of hundreds. I'm sure that you won't even consider me. This has the effect of making the person prove themselves of the chasing and saying, no, Of course we'll remember you. Of course you're different. It's almost like a playful version of emotional blackmail. And here's the thing. When they don't say anything, you know that you really don't think that you're special. And there's an objection there that you can handle. Again, remember that this version is just for more friendly or intimate situations.

For example, if you're a hedge fund manager trying to raise capital and you tell an institutional investor, oh, we're just another fund, I'm sure you won't even consider it special or even remember us. And I'm sure we're not even that good. Well, in that case, that's exactly what they may think. OK, what are some dos and don'ts with exclusion? Confirmation does qualify the person that this is for when possibly excluding them, make clear who this is for. And that will test better not just their commitment, but their traits and the client or as a target. Don't use this in a serious matter. This is supposed to be a lighthearted tactic to create intrigue.

If you're too serious, then the person will assume that they really are exquisite and this will backfire. So now that we've covered the theory of excluding or accusing the person, let's bring it back down to work and take a look at the specific examples of how to use it. What are some examples of exclusion confirmation? The first is false modesty. You don't want a friend to have something valuable to keep downplaying it, saying, oh, I have this opportunity, but I'm sure that you're not interested. I'm sure it's nothing special. They're using precisely this. Another example for accusations would be dating back in the day.

Some dating instructors would recommend a technique for the other person to remember you, which would be exactly this type of accusation, saying something like, oh, I'm just one of the first people that you met tonight. I'm sure you won't even remember me precisely to get them to chase. Another example is saying something is exclusive. What they're doing is precisely this. They're trying to exclude you, to bait you into chasing them. And if you don't, they probably have other people who will. This is used for entry in advance night clubs, conferences, restaurants and many others.

What are our use cases for the different quadrants in terms of marketing? You can build intrigue by saying I'm not sure if this product is for you. It's just for exclusive clients. Or if you're comfortable with a client, you can use accusation, for example, saying something like, oh, we're just another service provider to you, there are 300 like us, right, to get them to chase you on the personal. And you can build a tree with friends or even your kids saying something like, oh, I'm not sure that you want to come on this trip with us. Maybe you'll find it boring if you are comfortable again, you can use accusation. Oh, I'm sure you won't enjoy this vacation. It's just the same as others that we've done in the past.

On the corporate side, you can't exclude employees to create intrigue. Oh, I'm not sure this project is for you. It's just for very specific people or even your boss saying, oh, I know this proprietary technique from my best job to increase workload, but I'm sure you're not interested. And again, if comfortable, you can accuse, for example, with a friendly employee saying, oh, I'm sure I'm just another manager to you. All of us are the same to you. Right. Or on the fundraising side, you can use an exclusion type of entry. For example, you can say, oh, I'm not sure you want to invest in us. The startup is just for a particular type of VC or is an NGO. You can say, oh, I'm sure we're just another NGO on your list.

We're not even that special, are we? What are our key takeaways here? The first is that this is a version of a technique called into labeling, which forces the person to make something explicit here. We're using it in a kind of reverse manner. Usually you want the person to commit to something by making it explicit. Here, you're daring the person to make their exclusion explicit, which they want to do. So it has the opposite effect. Then we have accusations. A variation of this accusation relies on downplaying yourself and using false modesty to bait the other person into chasing and finding for you. Another takeaway is that this technique lends itself to exclusivity and mystique by saying something as, Oh, this is not for everybody.

You beat the person into chasing it. And finally, remember, it's not the end. So many clients and people tell me that they're afraid to use this technique because they are afraid of what will happen if the person doesn't actually chase, if they say it's not for me. And the key is that, well, first, if you've done everything right up to this point, they shouldn't. But even if they do, you just know that there is more work to be done in terms of persuasion. That's it. As we covered, excluding the person or even accusing them is a very powerful technique because this is supposed to create intrigue and to get the person to chase. And if they don't chase, then you know that there is something wrong there and there's an objection present.

What Next

Let's talk about presence, presence is probably one of the hottest and most talked about topics in both the communication, public speaking and persuasion in the streets, but at its core, regardless of the different components of presence, the core chapter is that if you're more intense, if you're a force of nature, if you are slow and you really have that intensity felt, you are going to persuade more. It's not due to intimidation, it's just due to presence itself. Of course, you can also intimidate, but at its essence you only need to be present with. Take a look at how being someone with intensity, presence and tension will persuade others more by itself.

Not because you are necessarily intimidating, but at least you have presence. You must be taken seriously by others. Now, naturally, as with many other techniques, there is no one key way to do this. But there are nine key pillars of presence itself. The first is charisma and salience just standing out. Then comes appearance in authority, looking the part after that intensity and tension itself. Eye contact, local tonality and so on. Then minimalism and collectivism. Doing less conveys more. When you speak less. When you move less, you communicate more power. After that rigidity, not tolerating a lot of people, then agency being someone who takes initiative when others don't.

Back to this synchrony being at peace with yourself, congruent activists, grace under pressure, not being affected by others or the environment in final vulnerability, being able to be open in terms of your emotions, your flaws in others. First comes charisma and salience in. These are all about standing up. You have your own version of the world, your story, your vision, and you influence others with that vision. Naturally, the stronger that it is, the more you influence it. This is cultivated by defining a crystal clear vision and fussing with it then becomes appearance in authority, in recovery, in brief framing.

But in this case, we don't use them to seem like an authority, but we use them to create tension and influence the other person. It's cultivated by having a selective creative image. If someone is very well dressed and looks very good, they just persuade more. After this comes intensity and tension. These are all about your actual cues about seeming serious, a force of nature. And this is cultivated by being intense in person, maintaining eye contact, having a stern tonality, using silence in being almost intimidating. After this comes minimalism and subjectiveness. These are hallmarks of confidence value. People are redundant, get off track, and high value people select their words and actions carefully.

This is cultivated by speaking class and doing less, but being intentional about every word, every gesture. After this comes rigidity. This is the equivalent of the personal rigidity in priming. It's you as a person in what you tolerate, what you do that from others. It's cultivated by demanding more from others, using personal boundaries to not accept anything that others may want, and not being easily satisfied, which communicates that you have standards both for yourself and for others. Agency is very simple. It's all about being a person of action. When someone is in a negative mood or when there's a problem to be solved, you don't avoid it like everyone else, but you tackle it head on.

This is just cultivated by practicing taking action on problems. Synchrony is all about being congruent, not being uncomfortable or feeling like something is not right with you. Using Amy Covey's definition, Synchrony is all about having all parts of yourself act as one. It's cultivated by, for example, being honest, because this honesty affects you physically being well rested and with good posture. Among other things, grace under pressure is all about not reacting emotionally. It's about keeping your cool even when provoked or attacked. As the saying goes, never let them see you sweat. And this is cultivated by simply not showing a reaction to events.

Vulnerability is all about not being afraid of showing emotion or even best. Which is, you've guessed it, inverse transparency. Often people don't fear sharing their own issues. It's cultivated by being open and not affected by things. What are some dos and don'ts of presence? Do work with what you have. Chances are you already have one strong pillar, one of these nine. It may be tension. It may be vulnerable before trying to cultivate all of the other ones and double down on what already works. Don't try to master all of these at the same time unless you're a truly assertive and intense person by nature.

This is because trying to make too many identity level changes at once can leave you kind of lost in the transformation. So now that we've taken a look at the nine key pillars of presence with all of its different dimensions, let's now take a look at how people actually leverage it in real life. What are some examples of presence? The first is a CEO meeting Wednesday where an employee of the company sits down with the CEO or another executive. They'll probably become paused or addressed minimalistic in their speaking and reacting. The second is frame battles. These are an example of two presences in conflict. For example, a sour as the frame that you need this product and you as the buyer may have the frame that you don't need them and they are the ones bothering you.

And the person with the most presence wins the frame battle and convinces the other person of reality. Lastly, figures of authority are another example. People such as policemen, military and other agents lamberton presence and questioning, using an aggressive tone, intense stares, silence, being dressed in expensive suits and more. What are our use cases for the different quadrants on the sales and marketing side? During conversations or presentations, you can simply have presence, be minimalistic, use eye contact, vocal tonality and others to convey strength. You can also not be affected by rejection tests or other attitudes.

For example, if a client talks about a weakness that you have and you freak out, they will assume there is something wrong. But if you remain calm, you will pass on a different impression of the personal and you can be intense with friends or in social situations using these same tools, eye contact, vocal tonality, etc.. You can also or should also not be affected by the emotional fluctuations of others, including family, because if they're emotional and you get emotional, you have less authority in the argument. But if you remain calm in what you say is a listen to more easily on the corporate end, you can be intense, use eye contact and so on when meeting your manager or employees.

And you can note here that bosses will have this by nature and employees want, but you can cultivate and even be better at it. I myself have had multiple bosses that would try to persuade through intimidation, but I would be calmer than they were with you as more eye contact than they would. And they would back down, not me. Now, you don't have to intimidate them, but you can be present enough to just not be intimidated yourself on the fundraising. And you can use Bretholz with possible investors, especially because in many situations they'll try to intimidate you. This is very frequent for an alternative asset manager. When receiving an allocation from an institution, the institutional CIO will play prosecutor and try to break you.

The goal is not to react and to just remain present with authority as normal. You can also remain calm and persist with investors or donors in general if they're trying to break you, if they try to intimidate you. EUPOL, we keep doing what you're doing and you are not affected by it. What are our key takeaways here? The first is that there are nine key pillars to presence. Although they see many, they are intimately related.

They are all about being a force of nature, having intensity being taken seriously. The second is that this works at the moment. While there are some components such as authority, reputation and image that do focus on the long term influence, presence is all about the here and now.

It's how much power you have as a person when you're looking someone else in the eyes. And finally, this presence is almost universal and influences how some people are self-confident and have the courage to challenge their inner self. What most people do as a reaction is just accept the presence and be persuaded, which is why this works so well. So as we saw, there are a whopping nine key pillars to presence. And here's the thing. You don't have to cultivate all of them. But if you just increase some of these dimensions of presence, you are going to have your actual presence felt in that interaction. You are going to have more strength in how you speak and how you act. And because of that, you persuade the person more easily.

What is Quality?

Let's start this topic by understanding what is quality. Before we go any further I would suggest that you stop this chapter here. Think about what your understanding quality means. You would have been the buyer, you would have been the supplier of a number of things. So think from that point of view what does quality mean to you. So then you think about quality. You think about quality in different ways for different products. Similarly when you ask a number of people about quality What is the definition of quality they will define quality differently from their own perspective. Lets say if you ask five people what is the definition of a good car, a good quality car. Someone might say that it needs to look good.

Someone might say that it needs to be fuel efficient. Someone might say that this needs to be reliable, depending on the needs of each of these individuals the quality definition will differ. So that's something which we need to recognize that quality has many definitions and another important thing is that quality is defined by the customer, not the manufacturer, not the designer, it's the customer who decides what quality is? So if a product or a service which you are providing meets the requirements, if that meets the expectations of that customer then the product is a quality product.

How to Define Quality? Seven Definitions of Quality.

After realizing the fact that quality has many definitions. Let's look at some of the common definitions related to quality. Quality could be defined as conformance to requirements, quality could be defined as fitness for use, meeting customers expectations, exceeding customers expectations, superiority to competitors and freedom from deficiencies. Each individual looks at quality from a different angle. In the next six chapters we will be looking at each of these six characteristics of quality one by one. So let's start with conforming to requirements in the next chapter.

Definition 1: Quality is Conformance to Requirements

So the first definition in this list of quality definitions is conformance, conformance to requirements. So quality means keeping the promises which were made at the time of taking order or what other commitments were made. If you keep those promises, that means your product or your service is a quality product. So if you take an example of an airline. So if you want to fly from airport A to airport B and you have a definite agreement, definite requirements where the airline is supposed to take off at this particular time, land at airport B at this particular time, allow you this many Kg of luggage, give you a hot lunch during the journey.

All these things are agreed requirements which were made when you booked that ticket. So if that airline meets these agreed requirements that means that airline is giving you a quality service instead of that if in the middle of the air you are told that you ordered for vegetarian food but we don't have vegetarian food that means it's not the quality service and the delay in airline, any inconvenience which were caused to you unexpectedly. All those things would count as poor quality service. So this is one definition of quality which is conformance to requirements. So in summary if your product or service meets the requirements then it is the quality product.

Definition 2: Quality is Fitness for Use

Another definition of quality is fitness for use. So it means that the product or service does what it is expected to do. So if you bought a pen the purpose of the pen was to write. If your pen is writing then it is a good quality pen. If it's not writing then it's not a good quality pen. So this definition of quality limits to the very basic minimum thing that the product or service that this was supposed to do at least that does that much, so this could be called quality. So here you need to recognize that if the product or service doesn't do what it was required to do then it might be costing something to the client, costing something to the customer that also needs to be taken into consideration. So for example in the case of an airline, if a flight from airport A to airport B gets delayed and because of that customer loses something, the customer loses the business, the customer loses the connecting flight, and the customer misses some opportunity. That is the cost of quality to the customer. So that needs to be avoided. When we say that quality means fitness for use.

Definition 3: Quality is Meeting Requirements

So the third and fourth definitions of quality are related to customer expectations, there might be some overlap between the conformance which we talked about earlier and expectations. Just to make the difference clear when I bought my vacuum cleaner which had five years of warranty, it worked for five years. So that means it conformed to the requirement, it conformed to the agreement but that was not my expectation that after five years and two months this vacuum cleaner will stop working. My expectation was that this vacuum cleaner which has worked five years would definitely be working for another five years so that was my expectation.

So even though this has met the conformance part of the quality but it has not met the expectations part so that's the difference between conformance and expectations. And when we say customer expectations that means quality is what customers say it is. So it's not the manufacturer, it's the supplier of the services or the product which decides whether the product is a quality product, it's the customer which decides based on what expectations they have from the product that customer or client will decide whether the product is a quality product or not. So this was about meeting expectations. Let's look at the next chapter and talk about exceeding customer expectations in that next chapter.

Definition 4: Quality is Exceeding Expectations

This definition of quality focus is on exceeding customers expectations. So the quality is the extent to which the product or service surpassed or exceeded the customers needs or expectations so that's how you define quality. The way it has exceeded or surpassed the customer's expectations when it comes to contractual situations. You might not want to use these clauses in your contract that your product or service would exceed clients expectations because these are all subjective things. So even though you don't want to put these things in your contract with the client. But in the background within the company you definitely would like to work to exceed customer's expectations. So once your product or service exceeds customers expectations that will lead to a delighted customer, that will lead to return orders, that will lead to more and more customer referrals. So that's something companies attempt to do to exceed customer's expectations and go above and beyond what was promised. So promise less and deliver more.

Definition 5: Quality means being Better than Competitors

The next definition in this chain of definitions is related to competitors. Quality is superiority to your competitors. How much better you are when compared to your competitors? That's what decides your quality. You cannot produce an ideal product or an ideal service. There could always be a chance to improve something. But when it comes to competitors how you stand against your competitors that's what will decide whether you'll sell the product or your competitor will sell the product to this particular customer. So this is another way to look at quality. How do you compare against your competitors?

Definition 6: Quality means being Defect Free

And the last definition in this chain of quality definitions is freedom from defects. Whenever you are making a product or providing a service your attempt would be to minimize defects. The problem with defects is that defects lead to rework and rework leads to more cost. So if you are producing a defective part that goes to the client then the problem would be that the client will be unsatisfied because it breaks, which leads to some failure. It led to some loss to the customer. So that's one scenario. Second scenario would be that you created a defect. Then you found that as a manufacturer then you repaired that the repairing of this product will cost you money.

So in either case you lose either you lose money in repairing or your customer loses the faith in your product. So defects need to be reduced or eliminated at any cost. So that is how you achieve quality. There is a general misconception that when you make a product which is free from defects that product is going to cost you more in manufacturing but you need to overcome that understanding. Once you make a product which is defect free you don't need to rework. You don't need to do a lot of inspections. You save a lot of money by not making defective parts.

So in a way in the long term not making defective parts will lead to improved profits. It's not going to cost you more. It's going to cost you less when you make defect free products. And in fact that will lead to consistency in your quality. So if you make defect free products you will make consistent quality, your customers will be happy and you will be getting the return orders. So these were six commonly used definitions of quality. None of these is an official statement that quality means this. So we need to have a common single definition of quality and who provides that definition. That definition is provided by ISO 9000 standard. So in the next chapter let's look at that official definition of quality. What does quality mean?

Definition 7: Quality as Defined by ISO 9000:2015

So here in this chapter we have the official definition of quality provided in ISO 9000-2015 standard and it defines quality as the degree to which a set of inherent characteristics of an object fulfills requirements. So when it says object it means product or service. So in plain and simple language what it means is your quality is compelling between that requirement and whether Briz requirements have been achieved or not. So there are certain inherent characteristics of each of the products or services which you provide.

So whether those inherent characteristics meet that requirement, that's what quality means. If the characteristics of the product or service meet the requirement then you have a good quality product. If the inherent characteristics of the product or service do not meet the requirements then the product or the services will require that people are a part service. So this is how you define quality. This completes our discussion on various definitions of quality. How do you define quality?

Difference between Quality and Grade

Previously when we were defining quality we talked about quality is about meeting requirements. So if the product or the service is meeting the requirements we will say that this product is a good quality product. So the quality of the product could be classified as poor, good or excellent. So this is something which we learned earlier. Now if I ask you a question, look at these two pens in this chapter, one on the left is a fountain pen with a golden tip. And the second one on the right is a one dollar ballpoint pen. So now my question is which of these two pens is a better quality pen.

When it comes to quality, a number of times people are confused about the difference between quality and grade. So when you are looking at two things when you're comparing two things. Look at that whether you are comparing quality or whether you are looking at two different grades. Here what I'm seeing is these two different grades. And when I say grades it's a different category of product. These two are not the same category of products. The purpose of both of these even though might be writing. But the overall purpose is not the same. The one on the left is a symbol of status. The second one on the right is just meant to write something.

One thing we should remember here is that when you're looking at quality make sure that you are not comparing two different things. You need to do apples to apples comparison rather than comparing two different grades. So now with this basic understanding of quality definitions and the difference between quality and grade. Now let's move on to the next chapter and look at the question why do we need quality.

Why Quality?

After looking at the definitions of quality. Now let's look at the reason why we need quality. This explanation of why quality was provided by Dr. Deming and this is also known as Deming Chain Reaction. So let's understand this. When you improve quality the first thing which will lead to less defects. So better quality means less defects. And when you have less defects that means your cost will go down because now you don't need to repair those problems, repair those defects. So better quality means low defects, low defects means lower cost. In addition to lower cost the better quality also helps in improving productivity because now there are less defects. There is less repair to be done. So all the time which you would have spent in repairing your product or service.

Now at the same time you can spend doing something more productive. So your productivity also goes up. So with these three things better quality, lower cost, high productivity. Your organization can capture the market because now with these things you have a competitive edge over your competitors and you can capture the bigger market because you have a better product, you have lower cost, your productivity is high. So this capture in bigger market share will help you in staying in the business.

And this in fact will lead to more jobs. So now we start with better quality and we end up with more jobs. So Deming was able to convince all the workers and people who were working in the organization to work towards better quality because better quality will protect their job. So this is why we need quality. Quality is good for the company. Quality is good for employees. Quality is good for customers, it's good for society. So better quality is good for all stakeholders.

Garvin's Eight Dimensions of Quality

Earlier when we were talking about Definitions of Quality one thing we understood was the quality has a different meaning for different people. To help overcome that problem of multiple definitions. Garvin has come with eight Dimensions of Quality. So when you look at these eight Dimensions of Quality look at these eight Dimensions has eight different types of lenses. So these are the lenses through which you see whether the product is a quality product or not. These Dimensions are a Performance, Feature, Reliability, Conformance, Durability, Serviceability, Aesthetics, and Perceived Quality. So these are different ways to look at Quality. Whatever product or service you are providing or whatever service or product you are purchasing look at that from these eight lenses and that will help you in defining the quality of that product or service. Let's go through each of these one by one and try to understand what does that mean. Let's start with Performance.

Performance (Garvin's Eight Dimensions of Quality)

The first Dimension in these eight Dimensions of Quality is Performance. Performance is the primary operating characteristic. This is the basic thing. This is the basic purpose of the product. Then we are trying to understand these eight Dimensions let's take an example of a car. If you are planning to buy a car how would you be looking at these eight Dimensions of Quality. So when it comes to Performance, the things which you will be looking at are the basic things, these are the basic requirements of that particular product. That's what you'll be seeing in performance. Most of the characteristics related to performance are measurable. You can measure when you're comparing two cars. You can compare these cars based on the engine size, based on the number of seats. All these things you can objectively compare with each other. That's a part of performance here.

Features (Garvin's Eight Dimensions of Quality)

The second Dimension of quality is Features, these Features are bells and whistles which are in addition to the primary requirement or the performance requirements. In case of the example of the car which we took this Feature could include examples such as the music system in the car, the heated seats and many other additional features which you get. So these extra things, these extra bells and whistles would fall under the Features Dimension of the quality.

Reliability (Garvin's Eight Dimensions of Quality)

The third Dimension of quality is Reliability. So in the example which we are talking about here , in the case of car Reliability means how much you can rely on this car not to fail when you are taking a critical trip. So that will be the Reliability of this, the Reliability could be seen based on the past performance. Some of your friends and family members would have bought that particular car and based on the failure history of that car you will make a belief that what is the Reliability of that car. So that's from the customer's perspective but from the manufacturer's perspective there are technical terms like mean time between failure, mean time for first failure. All those parameters are taken care of by manufacturers to make sure that the product or service which they are providing is Reliable.

Conformance (Garvin's Eight Dimensions of Quality)

The fourth Dimension of quality is Conformance. And this is related to meeting established standards, meeting requirements. These requirements could be internal which are set up within the organization or these standards could be external which are set up by the regulatory authorities or government. So let's say in the case of a car you have emissions standards that show how much emission this car will be producing. That's something which this car is supposed to meet. And then there are a number of internal standards established by the manufacturer that determine the tolerance in each of these components which are being assembled. So this is the fourth Dimension of quality which is related to meeting established standards.

Durability (Garvin's Eight Dimensions of Quality)

The fifth Dimension of Quality is Durability, Durability is the measurement of product life. How long this product is going to last. This might be somehow related to Reliability but there is a difference between Reliability and durability. Reliability is how frequently the product breaks and the Durability is how long this product is going to serve you. So in the example of a car you would like to have a car which is durable which can serve you for let's say 15, 20, or 25 years. So that's another Dimension of Quality.

Serviceability (Garvin's Eight Dimensions of Quality)

The sixth Dimension of Quality is Serviceability. This isn't related to speed, courtesy, competence and ease of repair. Things do go wrong. So even though there might be some issue with the reliability your car might fail at some time, this might need some repair. But then the next thing which you'll be concerned about as a customer would be the Serviceability. So here you will be looking at the speed, the courtesy, competency and the ease of repair. You don't want to wait for five days for your car to get repaired because they don't have spares in their service shop or you don't want to have incompetent people doing servicing. And Of course you'll be looking at the ease of repair, cost of repair and many other factors which are related to the servicing of the product.

Aesthetics (Garvin's Eight Dimensions of Quality)

So coming to this seventh Dimension of Quality which is an Aesthetics, this is the subjective Dimension of Quality. This is related to how a product looks, feels, sounds, tastes, smells; this is a personal judgment. So there's no hard and fast rule. So this is not something which is very objective, this is subjective and would differ from one person to another person. Some people might like the look of a particular car, some people might not like the look of that particular car. So this is a subjective Dimension but still this is an important Dimension of Quality. Since this particular Dimension of Quality is very subjective and it differs from person to person. It might not be easy for manufacturers or the producers to give a product which makes everyone happy. So this is one Dimension of Quality on which you might not be able to please all your customers.

Perceived Quality (Garvin's Eight Dimensions of Quality)

And this eighth and last Dimension of Quality is the Perceived Quality. This is the perception just like Aesthetics, Aesthetics was look, feel, taste. This Perception is just the mental Perception of a product or service. So when you talk of a car let's say Tesla you have a better Perception of the Quality when you talk of iPhone. You have a better Perception of Quality. So here in this particular Dimension of Quality the way you advertise, the way you pack your product, the way you deliver your product becomes very important. And just look at the iPhone how they advertise, how they deliver that product, their marketplaces, their brand image. All these things add up and give this particular aspect of quality which is the Perceived Quality.

So with this we complete the eight Dimensions of Quality. Now I would challenge you to look at the product or service which you are providing to your customers and go through each of these aspects and see how you deliver that product or service to your customer. So when you deliver a product. What are the Performance characteristics of that product? What are the main Features? What are the additional Features? What is the Reliability of that product, whether that product is Conforming to standards? What is the Durability, what is the Serviceability part of that? What is the Aesthetics ... the look, feel or smell? You might not be able to judge these things such as Aesthetics and Perception but you can always talk to your customer and see how they look and feel about your product. So do an analysis of all these eight Dimensions of Quality in regards to your own product or service that you are providing to your customers.

QA, QC and QMS - Intro

Previously we have talked about various definitions of quality and we have also talked about Garvin's eight dimensions of quality. Those things helped us in understanding what quality is but now the next question comes that how do we achieve quality. To put in a plain and simple language we achieve quality by ensuring that the client requirements are met. Or let's say the requirements are met, so you achieve quality by ensuring that requirements are met. And how do we do that? For ensuring quality we have various functions in quality. Let's understand those. So we have Quality Control. We are a Quality Assurance and Quality Management System. Many times people have confusion between the first two terms Quality Control and Quality Assurance. Let's learn that let's look at the difference and then we will understand what Quality Management System is. So this is what we are going to do in this chapter. Learn about these three terms. Quality Control, Quality Assurance and Quality Management System. Let's start with Quality Control.

Quality Control - Definition

So here is the definition of Quality Control. So when we say Quality Control it means that the operational techniques and activities used to fulfill requirements for quality. This might look a little bit difficult to understand but think of Quality Control as whatever you do to ensure that the requirements are met. That's quality control. So if you are making a product you make sure that all the input materials which you are receiving are of good quality. They meet that requirement and then you ensure that all the processes which are required to make those inputs to finish the products are being controlled and then you look at that final product probably this is what you do when you're making something. All the activities in this process to ensure that the requirements are met are quality control that's basically quality control and then the question comes then what's Quality Assurance. So let's look at that in the next chapter.

Quality Assurance - Definition

The definition of Quality Assurance is that all the planned and systematic activities implemented within the quality system that can be demonstrated to provide confidence that a product or service will fulfill the requirements for quality. And once again any official definition is sort of confusing so let's understand this as well. So the first thing in Quality Assurance is that we need to ensure that all the planned activities are implemented. So whatever we have planned for manufacturing that product, the product which we were talking about earlier. So whatever activities we plan we will make sure that those are implemented. We make sure that there is a system for doing all those things. The whole purpose of Quality Assurance is that this should be able to provide confidence that the product meets the requirement.

There are many ways to provide confidence, you can provide confidence to your management, confidence to your customers by ensuring that you have documented whatever activity you are doing. So in summary what our activities do to ensure your client, to ensure your management that the requirements are being met is Quality Assurance. And now let's go to the next chapter and look at the difference between Quality Assurance and Quality Control. There is an overlap between Quality Control and Quality Assurance. But then there are different focuses in each of these. So let's understand that in the next chapter.

Quality Control vs Quality Assurance

So here in this chapter we have the difference between QC which is Quality Control and QA which is Quality Assurance. So if you look at the first one the focus of Quality Control is on the product and that's what we were talking about when we looked at the definition also. The focus was on the product, The focus was on getting the right input. The focus was on getting the production done right and the focus was on making sure that the finished product meets the requirements. So in all that chain the focus was on the product whereas when it comes to Quality Assurance. The focus is on process. So here the intent is that if the processes are being done in the right way the product will be right. In QA the focus is on the process.

Coming to QC, QC is considered to be reactive. Q is considered to be proactive. So in QC you look at the product if you see the problem then you attend to that problem and make sure that the problem is not repeated. So basically all these activities happen once you have a problem whereas in QA you make sure beforehand that your processes are set so that you don't get into trouble. So that's the focus of QA being proactive. QC is the line function and QA is the staff function. So when you say line function and the staff function, line function is something which is let's say in case of production. These QC people report to the production group. Here the focus is on production. QC is working in the shop. QA is a staff function. This is a support function.

The next one here is that the focus of QC is on finding defects whereas the focus of QA is on preventing defects This is somewhat similar to what we said when we said reactive and proactive. Coming to this fifth line where we said that QC is related to Testing and QA is related to Quality audits. So the tools used for Quality Control is the testing, testing is the tool for Quality Control and audits are the tools for

Quality Assurance function. So this chapter gives you a difference between these two aspects of Quality, Quality Control and Quality Assurance. Having understood this now let's move to the next thing which is the quality management system.

Quality Management System

So if I look at the definition of Quality Management System in ISO 9000. The definition of Quality Management system is that this is a part of Management System with regards to Quality. So it's a very general definition here. So let's try to understand what a Quality Management System is. So Quality Management System is a formalized system that documents the structure, responsibilities and procedures required to achieve effective quality management. If you remember earlier in QA also we talked about processes. This is what. QAM is QMS to make sure that we have documented processes for whatever work we are doing. We have processes, we are structures, we have responsibilities, all these things become part of the Quality Management System. In a typical organization if you look at the Quality Management System.

This forms a sort of pyramid, at the top of the pyramid is the Quality Policy, Quality Policy gives the overall direction in regards to quality. Then the next layer in this hierarchy is the Quality Manual, Quality Manual gives the high level overview of all the processes being followed in the organization. Next layer comes the Procedures, Procedures give details related to who is doing what, where all those details are available in Procedures. Then the next layer in this hierarchy would be Work Instructions. Work Instructions are basically more details when it comes to procedure more details are provided in Work Instructions those even go to minute details. And tell how each of these activities is being performed. And at the bottom of this hierarchy is records.

Records are basically the evidence which tell that these processes have been performed as these were planned. So if you look at any organization typically they will have this sort of hierarchy. They might have a different name. Some organizations may have the term quality manual. Some might not have that. And there have been some changes in this structure earlier prior to ISO 9001 2015. The latest version of ISO 9001 was issued in 2015. Prior to that there was a requirement to have a quality manual. So all the organizations which are certified to ISO 9001 standard were required to have a quality manual.

But after 2015 addition that requirement has been taken out. So some organizations still might have a quality manual, some organization might have this quality manual in some other form. But this is something which tells at the top level how things work in an organization. So this basically is the typical structure of the Quality Management System in an organization. So in this chapter we have talked about Quality Control. We have talked about Quality Assurance. We looked at the difference between QC and QA. And we understood what the Quality Management System is. Together these things help us in achieving quality in our organization.

Now so far we have learned about what is Quality, we learned about the Dimensions related to Quality the eight Dimensions given by Garwin and we understood some key terms related to quality. QA QC and QMS were something which were required to implement quality. Before we go any further in this Book, why don't we just go back and look at the history of quality. I am not going into the details of that. But I just want to give you a glimpse of how things have moved till today in regards to quality, how things changed, and how new concepts were developed. Let's have a quick look at the history of quality before we go any further.

Brief History of Quality

In this chapter we will look at the history of quality. I am not going into the details of each and every activity whatever has happened. I would just give you a glimpse of things which have happened in these 100 plus years in regards to quality management. Somewhere around 1900 industrial expansion was happening and that led to more focus on quality. Somewhere around 1910 Frederick Taylor introduced the principle of scientific management which in fact was related to time and motion studies.

Coming to the 1920s Walter Shewhart introduced the concept of statistical process control SPC and control charts. Even though these things were introduced in 1920 but these were not much in use till 1940 1946. The American Society for Quality was established at that time. The name of this organization was the American Society for quality control. But later on the name changed to ASQ which is American Society for Quality. 1950 to 1960 is considered to be the golden era for quality management. Lots of things have happened in that time 1950 or 1960 and much of the credit goes to Japan because many of these things were focused in Japan.

This was the time when Joseph Juran published his first edition of quality control handbook and this was the time when Juran and Deming were invited to Japan for helping in improving the quality. Deming has taught a number of people, a number of Japanese engineers on statistical process control and quality and at the same time Feigenbaum introduced the concept of quality cost driven recovering the concepts related to quality cost in this Book coming to 1960. Ishikawa introduced 7 quality tools of quality. These seven tools of quality were taught to each individual in the organization so that with the help of these very common tools people can improve quality.

So these seven quality tools are still considered to be the one of the important things in quality management and I will be introducing these 1:53 of quality in the schools as well as we move farther into the schools. Ishikawa also introduced the concept of quality circles. The concept of quality was a goal where people who are working on a particular area sit together and look at the improvement opportunity using the 7 quality tools midday improvement. So this was basically delegating power to individuals who are working to make a quality circle is still considered to be one of the important aspects of achieving quality in Japan.

In 1979 Philip Crosby who is also considered to be one of the important quality gurus in the field of quality management published his first book which was quality is free and that raises the awareness of quality in Western society. In 1986 Motorola introduced the concept of Six Sigma Six Sigma was used to improve the quality of the product. Our process is to a very high level very high level where the level of defect was 3.4 diffract million opportunity. So that was the start of a level which was being achieved using the Six Sigma approach. I have a number Of courses related to six sigma on you.

When you go for six sigma you go through a number of bags and these bags are related to the level of your competency. You start with six sigma whitebait then you go for six sigma yellow belt then you go for six sigma green belt and next is six sigma black belt. So you follow this hierarchy and go through the processes of improving quality. So this concept was introduced in 1986 by Motorola coming to 1987. This was the first time ISO-9001 was introduced. ISO 9001 provides a structure to establish the quality management system. So earlier we have a good quality management system where we say that it's sort of a hierarchy at the top you have quality policy.

Then you have quality manual procedures, work instructions and records. That concept was emphasized by ISO 9000. So here you are required to establish a set of processes that demonstrate that and get certified. So 1987 ISO 9000 was published for the first time. This was the first edition of ISO 9001. Coming to 1988 and 1991 this was the time when business excellence models were introduced. These are also called quality awards. 1988 Malcolm Baldrige National Quality Award. So this is the award given to American industry. This was established which has a set of processes which you need to work through.

To claim this quality of Wired 91 utopian foundation for quality management they introduce their own model of business excellence. Moving to 2000 it is said that nine thousand one was introduced in 1987 and then it went to revision from 1987 to 1994 the year 2000 was the third revision. And 2000 it was the fourth version of ISO nine thousand one and 2015 is the fifth or the latest version of ISO-9001. So this gives the brief history of what all has happened in this process. Number of things have come. I have not covered the TQM. The concept of TQM also came for some time. The concept of lean to lean manufacturing is still a very important part of quality management.

So if you look at the few key aspects in quality management on Isel 901. So if you are related to quality management you probably need to know ISO nine thousand one you need to know about lean manufacturing lean processes. You need to know about six sigma. You need to know about analysis that is fact because there is so much data analysis being done today. So this is where we stand in regards to quality today. So this covers the quick introduction to the history of quality.

Quality Gurus

In the previous chapter we talked about the History of Quality. In that history we talked about Edwards Deming. We talked about Juran, we talked about Philip Crosby. In the chapter let's look at the works of these Three Quality Gurus. There are a number of people who have contributed to the field of quality. Many of those are called Quality Gurus but we're focusing our discussion only on these three quality gurus which are Deming Juran and Crosby. Let's understand the key teachings of these quality gurus and see what we can use or adopt in our own work or in our organization. Let's start with Edwards Deming first.

Edwards Deming

Before we look at the works or the teachings of Edwards Deming, let's quickly look at his life. Deming received his Ph.D in Mathematical Physics and he worked in Western Electric. He was a professor of statistics and he taught Quality Control to Japanese in 1950. So when in 1950 the Japanese industry was suffering. Dr. Deming was invited to teach about the quality of statistics in Japan. At that time Dr. Deming and Juran were also later invited to improve the industry in Japan. So in 1950 he started working in Japan and just after a year Japan established the Deming prize in his name. So any industry, any company who is doing good in the field of quality was given the Deming prize and the Deming prize was an honor to the works of Demming which he did to improve the quality of Japanese industry.

So after working for a long time improving the Japanese quality. Dr Deming gave an interview to NBC and the title of that interview was "if Japan can, why can't we?" And this was basically focused on US industry telling them that if Japan was destroyed by war. If they can do that if they can take their quality level to such a height why can't American industry do that. So if you are interested in this interview you can find this interview on YouTube. So this was a brief introduction to Dr. Deming. In the next chapter let's look at some of his teachings.

Deming is best known for

So here in this chapter I have the key teachings given by Dr. Deming. Let's quickly go through the list first. The first one is Deming's quality chain reaction. And if you remember earlier when we talked about why quality at the very beginning of this Book. Why do we need quality? That was basically Deming's Quality Chain Reaction and this was telling that if you improve quality if you do good work that will lead to more jobs. So that was something which we have already covered. In this chapter we will be covering these 14 principles of management which Deming proposed to Western industry. We will go through each of these and see what you can do to improve the quality or the level of your organization. We will go through each of these 14 points or each of these fourteen principles, then Deming talked about a system of profound knowledge.

He talked about the seven deadly diseases and he talked about variation, common cause and special cause. This was basically something which you see in control charts, control charts tell you when you should take action and then you should not take. So if the variation is because of Common Cause there is no need to panic. There's no need to take action. And if the variation is because of a special cause then you need to take action. Management should be aware of this concept because taking too many actions quickly reacting to any change basically will make the situation worse. So that's what Deming was proposing: that you need to understand the difference between the common cause and the special cause.

Take action and the special cause. Because then only your action is meaningful. He also talked about the Red Bead Experiment. We are not going through each of these items, we have already seen Deming's quality chain reaction and in this chapter we will be just focusing on 14 principles of management. These are very important principles. Listen to them and see how you can implement that in your organization. So let's move on to the next chapter and start looking at these 14 principles of management. 32. Deming's 14 Principles of Management We will discuss each of these in next 14 chapters: Create constancy of purpose for improving products and services.

Adopt the new philosophy. Cease dependence on inspection to achieve quality. End the practice of awarding business on price alone; instead, minimize total cost by working with a single supplier. Improve constantly and forever every process for planning, production and service. Institute chapter on the job. Adopt and institute leadership. Drive out fear. Break down barriers between staff areas. Eliminate slogans, exhortations and targets for the workforce. Eliminate numerical quotas for the workforce and numerical goals for management. Remove barriers that rob people of pride of workmanship, and eliminate the annual rating or merit system. Institute a vigorous program of education and self-improvement for everyone. Put everybody in the company to work accomplishing the transformation.

Principle # 1: Create Constancy of Purpose

So let's look at these 14 principles one by one. These 14 principles are for management, management to make sure that your company has competitive advantages, and your company's successes in the long term. So that is the purpose of these fourteen principles. And the first principle here is to Create Constancy of Purpose. Any organization should clear the constancy of purpose towards improvement of product or service with the aim to become competitive and stay in business to provide jobs. So here in this first point what Deming is proposing is that organizations should have a long term vision long term purpose rather than just looking at the quarterly report, just focusing on three months profit rather than that organizations need to have a long term vision. Without that vision you really cannot succeed as an organization and the organizations should invest in innovation, chapter, research with all these things they can improve their competitive position. That's something which all great companies have. So this is the first and the most important thing in these fourteen principles of management.

Principle # 2: Adopt the New Philosophy

The second management principle proposed by Dr. Deming is Adopt the New Philosophy. One thing you should remember is that these principles were proposed way back, let's say around 1980 or something around that period. So it's not something which has been proposed today. So it's already 30-40 years old principals. At that time Deming was saying that management needed to adopt the new philosophy. You really cannot work on your old way of working, the old style of working. Management needs to change. That's something Deming was proposing as a second principle of management that management needs to adopt new philosophy because things are changing.

The economy is changing and at this point he was focusing on Western management, saying that the Western management needs to take on challenges and must learn responsibility and lead for change. Because you really cannot improve if you are not ready to change. So be prepared for change. Look at how you can improve customer satisfaction, what are the changes you need to make to make sure that your company provides the customer satisfaction for that you might have to train your people, invest in all new technology or whatever you need to do. You need to make sure that you adopt new philosophy changes as things are changing, so that was point number two given by Dr Deming.

Principle # 3: Cease Dependence on Mass Inspection

Third management principle provided by Dr. Deming was Cease Dependence on Mass Inspection. Inspection is not a solution to quality. You need to have quality built into your processes. If you are just relying on 100 percent inspection, 200 percent inspection that's not going to help you. Inspection is not the solution to quality. Quality is achieved by putting things into processes. If you have the right processes you will achieve the right product, whatever inspection levels you have you will still have defective pieces, you will still have quality problems. So if you really need to achieve quality look beyond inspection because inspection might not help you.

So your processes should be such that whatever you produce, whatever service, whatever product you're producing, you should be able to produce the right product the first time that should be your attempt rather than making something and then inspecting and sorting that out as a good product or the bad product rather than that work on improving your processes so that you make the right thing first time. That was point number three or principle number three provided by Dr. Deming.

Principle # 4: Don't Award Business on the Basis of Price

The fourth principle for management provided by Deming was don't award business on the basis of price. You would see a number of places where if you want to buy something you ask for three bids and then you award that particular item to the lowest bidder. That's the general convention even today, Deming was totally against that. His point was that we should not be awarding business just based on the price tag. Rather it should be on the minimum total cost because the price is the one thing which you pay straight away. But then on top of that if we have to do some repair, if you are to do some re-work, if you have to do some extra things on top of that.

You need to consider all those aspects when you are awarding something not just on that single price tag that whichever is providing lowest you buy from that. You need to consider the lifetime cost of that item which you are buying. So that was one part of this. The second part here is that award to a single supplier. Many people did not like this or did not really understand this aspect of management that you don't buy from multiple sources because there is a general psychology. Like if I want to buy one product, I am manufacturing some part and let's say I want to buy nuts and bolts for that which I will use for assembling that.

Me as a manufacturer will think that I need to buy from three or four different places so that these people compete against each other. I get the lowest price. But one thing which we should remember here is that when you are buying from three or four different places just because you are buying from the three or four places because you just want to be sure that if something happens to one supplier you still have your supply. That was the reason to have multiple suppliers. One thing is that you think that you will get a consistent supply even if there is a problem with one supplier.

The second was that you would get things cheaper but what happens is that when you buy a product from multiple sources one thing you are doing is you are introducing too much of the variation into your processes because now nuts and bolts provided by three different suppliers might have different dimensions. Different levels of controls so that way I'm introducing inconsistency in my product. So that was one aspect of that, second aspect which Demming proposed was that if you're buying from a single supplier then you can have a long term relationship with that particular supplier, long term relationship means you can really go into the production of that particular supplier. See how they are controlling that if you want to change something you can change that because that's a long term relationship not just a one time purchase because if you're buying from one supplier that will be really happy to change whatever you need to make you happy because you're buying in bulk now.

So if you're buying in bulk you get things cheaper as well. So there are a number of benefits if you are buying one product from one supplier rather than looking for multiple suppliers who are competing against each other. And when they compete against each other definitely they will be compromising on quality as well because if they are competing on price somewhere they will start cutting corners So instead of going into that price war, instead of going into multiple suppliers look for a single supplier for each product. With that supplier establish a long term relationship so that you get a consistent product at a bulk rate. So this was Principle Number four provided by Dr. Deming.

Principle # 5: Improve Constantly and Forever

Principle number five is Improve Constantly and Forever. That's easy to understand. Very simple basic concept that there is no end to improvement. You can keep on improving. You really cannot make something perfect. There is always a scope, there is always the chance to make things better, so keep looking for improvement ideas. Keep improving whatever product or service you are making. By improving not only you improve the quality you reduce the cost as well and that's what we talked earlier in Why quality also as you improve your defect rate goes down. If your defect rate goes down that means the rework goes down, the cost which you are spending on the work will go down, your productivity will improve.

There are lots and lots of benefits in improving quality and that's what this Point Number Five says that keep on improving. For improving one approach suggested by Demming was and which was Of course based on the previous knowledge use PDCA approach. PDCA is plan, do, check and act. So this is a cycle where you plan something. Then you do that thing and then you check whether you have done it right or not. And then based on that checking you act, act means if whatever change you need to make make those changes. So you keep on working on this PDCA cycle you plan, do, check, act again plan, do, check, act. So this is a continuous cycle that can help you in continuously improving whatever you are doing.

And in that process make sure that you engage everyone, all employees engaged in this improvement process. So when it comes to improvement Demming always was looking for reducing variation because variation is an enemy of quality. If you have too much variation your quality will go down. So make sure that you are working on variation and whatever product we are doing, whatever service you are providing. Make sure that you reduce variation because if you reduce variation you will be consistently providing the right or the good quality of product or service. So this was a point about five Improve Constantly and Forever.

Principle # 6: Institute chapter on the Job

The sixth principal provided by Deming was the Institute chapter on the Job. chapter is important. So when you want to improve something you need to train because if you want to engage all the employees then you need to train them. You need to train them so that all your employees are able to identify where things are going wrong, where there is an opportunity to improve. And if they find the opportunity to improve. They need to have resources, they need to have skill to make those changes, to solve those quality problems. You need to train your people, when it comes to chapter out of these 14 points there'll be another point which is related to chapter. Here in this Point Number six Deming is talking about the job chapter, chapter related to whatever thing people are doing.

Then later on you will see that there's another one more principle related to chapter. Where Deming would say that you need to even expand beyond what you are doing. People need to be trained beyond what is happening right now. But at this point let's stick to the chapter related to the job. Two people need to know how they can do the job right, how they can find out the problem, and how they can solve it. So companies need to put some money into their employees. So this was principle number six provided by Deming which is the Institute chapter on the Job.

Principle # 7: Institute Leadership

Point number seven or the 7th the principal provided by Dr. Deming was Institute Leadership. When you talk of leadership and when you talk of supervision we need to understand that the role of the leadership or the supervision is to support people below them not be policemen, not to be pushing people to do more... do more... Rather than that, they need to understand what problems people have. People are working under them, what problems they have and how they can support them to overcome those problems. That should be the role of leadership and that's what needs to be understood in the organization that leadership needs to support people below them. Support people, support machines, support gadgets whatever things are there in the process make sure that they do the better job.

And another important aspect here is that the leadership or supervisors need to understand processes. If they don't know the processes they're not here just to push people to do more more more if they don't understand the process. So really they cannot help in improving those processes. They really cannot help people working on those processes, so supervisors need to be aware of processes for that they need to put their foot down, go to the workplace, look at things, what's happening, what's going wrong. So the need to get involved in processes not just become the supervisor to make sure that you achieve the daily quota. That's not the purpose of supervisors, supervisors need to understand the process, and need to provide all the support which people, machines, or gadgets need to make sure that the right product is being produced. So that should be instituted in the organization that the role of leadership is not to be a policeman but it is to support the processes, support people.

Principle # 8: Drive Out Fear

The principal number eight is Driving out Fear, a very important principle here. People need to be free from fear. So if I have a problem I should be free to tell that to my supervisor, if I see that something is going wrong. I shouldn't be able to freely tell that to my supervisor without being afraid that something which organization needs to have. People need to be fearless to tell something to improve something because if people are afraid, if I am afraid to tell my supervisor that things are going wrong then what good is that for the organization. And that can be achieved by mutual respect between the management and the worker. So if there is no mutual respect between these two you really cannot have a fear free environment. So you need to establish a fear -free environment. That's not something which can happen overnight. That happens based on the incidents.

People look at things how management reacts to workers complaints, how management reacts to workers pointing out something wrong. People see that. So once people see that, once people see that management is supportive, management thinks that if a worker is pointing out something wrong that's good for the organization. If that's the way management thinks then workers will be more inclined, workers will be more fear free to tell the process to improve quality. So this is a very important aspect that in an organization where you are looking for improvement there should be an environment where people can talk to each other freely without being afraid of losing the job, without being afraid of any consequences. So that's something which is very important and needs to be implemented. So this was point number eight presented by Dr. Deming in those 14 principles which is Drive Out Fear.

Principle # 9: Break Down Barriers

Principle Number nine in this list is Break Down Barriers. Many organizations if you look around will have a different silo. Each department, each function works in their own silo. Sales is just interested in selling the product without knowing how to make it. How does this organization produce that? The design group produces that design without thinking how this will be manufactured, the manufacturing or the fabrication department works in its own silo. They want to make change. They won't go back to design. You will see a number of organizations where each department or each function works in its own silo without talking to each other. That is the one of the biggest problems when it comes to quality, when it comes to organizational improvement. So what Deming is proposing in this Point number nine is that Break Down Barrier, break down barriers between different departments, different functions so that people work together as a single team.

And if you remember the point number one was to have a long term vision. So if everyone is working towards a long term vision as a single team that is the recipe to success for any organization. So in this concept we need to make sure that we build an environment in the organization where each function in the chain considers the next function in the chain as internal customers so that they serve the next internal customers best. And that way the whole chain works and the quality of the organization improves. And if you have a problem then rather than working on that problem in a silo there shouldn't be multi discipline or the cross-functional teams which work on that problem and solve that problem in the best interest of everyone rather than just looking from the point of view of their own department, from the point of view of their own function. So this is something which organizations need to implement if they really need to improve the quality of their product or service which is Break Down Barriers between departments or functions.

Principle # 10: Eliminate Numerical Goals, Posters and Slogan

Come into this tenth point given by Deming which is Eliminate Numerical Goals, Posters and Slogans. So basically slogans assume that the quality problem is because of people not because of the system but the fact is whatever problems you are having those are because of the system that you have. You need to improve the system rather than blaming people for those problems. Putting slogans indirectly tells that the problem is because of people. When you tell people to make sure that you make things right, what you are assuming is that people are not doing the right thing. So that's what Deming is suggesting in this point number ten that we need to Eliminate Numerical Goals, Posters, Slogans and when I say numerical goals.

That means looking at a zero defect, motivational posters, slogans because all these things mean nothing whatever problems and issues your organization is having. Most of these are because of the system , not because of people who were working on those systems. So if your organization sets a target of zero defect, put all those nice motivational posters around the factory, asking workers to work towards zero defect and since the problem is because of the system, workers will not be able to achieve zero defect. What indirectly that will lead to is a worker de- motivation because workers know that they need to make a zero defect but they are not able to produce zero defect that in fact will lead to demotivation in workers. So this was point number ten given by Deming.

Principle # 11: Eliminate Numerical Quotas

The 11th principal provided by Demming is Eliminate Numerical Quotas. Many people might not be able to digest this statement that we don't need to have a Quotas. But the fact is most of the time whatever Quotas or the production target companies have. That's just arbitrary. So these numbers are most of the times arbitrarily or at the maximum these might be looking at the pass production and let's say adding 10 percent to that. Last month we produced 100 pieces. So that's a target of hundred and ten pieces for this month. Those sorts of things are there when it comes to quotas, Deming was in favor of eliminating quotas on the production floor and substitute that by leadership.

Leadership to make sure that whatever we produce we produce of excellent quality, we work towards achieving customer satisfaction that sort of I think we should be looking for rather than just putting a number and people working towards that number. So if you have a target to produce 100 pieces today you will get 100 pieces. Forget about the quality. Forget about other things. But if you set a target people will what's target rather than looking at the long term perspective, looking at how they can improve processes, how they can improve quality, how they can improve customer satisfaction rather than that people will be just focusing on whatever number targets has been set because they know this is the number based on that they will be evaluated. So this was point number 11 Eliminate Numerical Quotas.

Principle # 12: Remove Barriers to Pride in Workmanship

The next point which is point number twelve given by Deming is that Remove Barriers to Pride in Workmanship. And what does that mean is Deming says that removing barriers that robs hourly workers and management of their right to pride of workmanship. What does that mean? People need to be proud of whatever they are doing. When we put people against each other. And the classic case of that is annual merit rating where we rate each individual based on a number of factors. So when you rate people based on a number of factors, what does that mean? Basically what they are doing is you are comparing people against each other. You are competing with people. So the result of that is people compete against each other. They are not team workers.

Because here an individual wins at the end of the day, at the end of the year when you're looking for the increment and that increment is based on your merit score, to get that score what you need to do is you need to be better than others that what you actually need to do. And what does that mean is that you don't need to be a team player. So what this annual rating does is basically this destroys the team environment because here people are rated individually. So people compete against each other. There is no question of having teamwork.

There's no question of having pride in what people do as a part of that organization as a whole organization. Here what matters is how people do individually if you have a merit system. So Deming was against having a merit system, Deming was against having anything which let people compete against each other rather than working together towards the common objective. So this is the twelfth principle provided by Deming which is Remove Barriers to Pride in Workmanship.

Principle # 13: Education & Rechapter

So coming to this thirteenth principle provided by Deming which is Education and Rechapter and if you remember in six the principal principal number six we didn't talk about on the job chapter where people were required to be taught how to do whatever they are doing. Here the emphasis is different even though both of these are related to chapter but emphasis here is on Education and Rechapter. Here what Deming asked was to have a program of education and self improvement. The scope of this principle is not just limited to the job chapter. The scope of this particular principal which is principal number 13 is to have a program of education and self improvement where people can learn new skills. Things are changing drastically so you need to have your workforce which is ready to take future challenges. So this was point number 13 that you need to educate or provide a chapter to your employees.

Principle # 14: Take Action

If you remember when we started talking about these 14 principles we started with principles number one which was management having a vision of that future. So you'll start the Vision and you end with that Action. So this is where point number 14 takes us. Take Action management needs to take action, management needs to make changes. Start making cultural changes so that people work towards these fourteen principles. Initially people will be skeptical about these changes. Many of these initially look controversial. For example if I ask you to just work with one particular supplier for one product. If people have worked with multiple suppliers they might be reluctant to make that change. People might be reluctant to change that thinking that we need to abolish our annual rating system, employee rating system.

Some of these are really a big challenge. If you really want to make a big change, go through all these 14 principles and start implementing them. So organizations who really want to make a big change need to work on all these 14 principles. It's not a question of picking and choosing. You might pick some changes and you might want to ignore some of those. That's really not going to help you if you really want to make a big change. Look at all these 14 principles that work towards achieving them. It might take time but in the long run this really will take your organization to the next level. Using these 14 principles a lot of Japanese companies have changed. They have become world class organizations. So will be your company if you look at these principles sincerely and start implementing them.

Joseph Juran

Previously we talked about Edwards Deming. We briefly looked at the life of Deming and then we looked at how Deming works and we have gone into detail of 14 principles provided by Dr. Deming. Now let's move on to the next big quality guru who is Joseph Juran. If we just look at the history of Joseph Juran, a very brief history here. Somewhere around the 1920s Juran joined Western Electric and in 1951 Juran published his quality control handbook. Today if you think a quality control handbook might not be a big deal. But look at 1951 where quality was not really that mature a subject that Handbook has really changed a lot. That has led people to understand what quality means.

So that was the time Juran published his first hand book quality control handbook. This has gone through a number of revisions and every few years you get a new version of that. If you are really considering a career in quality management this is the one book which you must have. Go to Amazon Dot Com and order this book. This is a thick book. This might cost you around let's say one hundred and fifty dollars but it is absolutely worth that. Just like Dr. Deming, Dr. Juran also taught Japanese about quality and that was around the 1950s just in the similar timeline when Deming was teaching Japanese people. Juran was also there teaching quality to Japanese. So this was a brief history of Dr. Joseph Juran.

Not coming to the key Contributions of Dr. Juran. Here in this chapter I have listed ten steps of quality improvement. We will go through that in the next chapter. And we have already talked about the quality control handbook published by Juran that is basically a reference for any quality professional. Juran has also proposed the Juran trilogy. We will talk about that. Juran was in favor of top management involvement and we understand that without top management involvement you really cannot achieve quality. Juran emphasized on Pareto principle. Pareto principle is eighty twenty principle in the context of quality Pareto principle means that by solving twenty percent issues just by solving top 20 percent issues we can eliminate 80 percent of the problems.

So this was heavily supported by Juran. So Juran's definition for quality was fitness for use. As we move further and we talked about Philip Crosby, Philip Crosby's definition for quality is different. Phillip Crosby considers the quality as conformance to requirements. So we were talking about Phillip Crosby after we covered Joseph Juran but each quality guru has emphasized different things in regards to quality. So the definition proposed by Juran was that quality is fitness for use. If the product or service which you are using is good for the purpose then this is a quality product so that's what Juran proposed.

Another important teaching of Juran was the project-by- project approach of quality improvement. The Six Sigma approach of quality is project- by- project improvement and that's what Juran proposed. So this is a brief listing of contributions of Dr. Joseph Juran and what we will do is we will look at two of these things in a little bit more detail. The first is ten steps of quality improvement and then later on we will talk about the Juran trilogy. So let's understand these two things in this Book, ten steps of quality improvement and the Juran trilogy. Let's start with ten steps in the next chapter.

10 Steps to Achieve Quality by Juran

When it comes to quality improvement, a number of people have emphasized different approaches. If you look you will see that there is an approach called PDCA for any improvement. The first thing which you need to do is plan, then do, and then check, and then act. So that's one cycle of quality improvement. If you look at some other places, let's say on six sigma, in a six sigma field you have a DMAIC approach. DMAIC is Define, Measure, Analyze, Improve and Control. So you will see different approaches to quality improvement at different places. Here let's look at 10 steps provided by Dr. Juran when it comes to quality improvement.

You'll start with building awareness for the need and opportunity for improvement. The first thing which you need to do is make a case for your improvement and then you set the goals. Then you organize and reach the goal, provide chapters to people, carry out projects to solve problems, and report the progress. Once you have done, once you have made an improvement then you report the progress, give recognition, communicate results to everyone or all the concerned people and then keep the score of improvements achieved. So you make a list of what all you have improved and then keep momentum.

So these are the 10 steps provided by Juran, you really cannot achieve improvement without a proper plan. And that's what this plan gives you. If you want to achieve improvement you need to follow these 10 steps or you follow DMAIC or you follow PDCA or you follow the 8D approach. Or you might consider these 10 steps so that's all your choice. So with this we complete the discussion on the 10 steps of quality improvement provided by Dr. Juran.

Juran's Trilogy

Earlier when we talked about the achievements of Dr. Juran, one of the items in that was the Juran trilogy. This is what Juran suggested. Let's understand that. Quality is achieved in three main stages. The first one is quality planning. So whatever product or service that you are making, the first thing that you need to do is to do quality planning. How do you plan to achieve quality and based on that you achieve a certain level of quality. So here if you look at this diagram on the bottom right here I have the picture given by Dr. Juran how he demonstrated the trilogy, how he demonstrated the achievement of quality. This is the quality planning part, based on this quality planning you do quality control.

So you start making the product or you start providing the service and you achieve a level of quality here. So this is what is demonstrated as quality control where you achieve quality within certain boundaries. You really cannot achieve a certain number. Sometimes your numbers will go up. Sometimes your numbers will go down. This is because of natural fluctuation. So if you have a repair rate mentioned here for example then some day you will have a slightly higher repair rate, some day slightly lower rate but then you'll still have a band within which your production is working because you have quality control in place.

So this is stage number two which is quality control which means meeting goals during operation. But then what happens is at a certain stage you go through quality improvement processes. You make a breakthrough improvement. Once you make that breakthrough, your level of quality improves in a single step and that's what is shown here. So the level of quality improvement means your defect level goes down and that's what is demonstrated here by a downturn here that the quality gets improved. And then once you improve the quality and then you have a new level of quality control, so the quality control band that you had here earlier now your quality control band is here at the bottom at a lower ejection rate.

Based on whatever quality improvement you're doing you'll learn something. And this is what the feedback cycle is: that you learn something and you feed it back to your planning portion. So you again plan, you again do the quality control, you again make some improvement. And this cycle of improvement continues. And here if you see that even though you're in control, there might be some cases where you might have a spike. Once in a while you might have some fluctuation, some uncontrolled thing, something might happen and that might give this sort of a spike but then generally you control within these quality control limits. This is the way to achieve quality as a Quality Trilogy.

So anyway if you want to achieve the quality you've planned for, you control that and then you make breakthrough improvements and learn from that. And then again plan so this cycle of improvement continues. So this was another item which I want to discuss here which is the Juran Trilogy. So with this we complete our discussion about Dr. Juran. 51. Transcript So far we have talked about Dr. Deming and we have talked about Dr. Juran both of these have made their name by improving the quality in Japan. Now let's move on to the third main quality guru which is Philip Crosby. Philip Crosby did not earn his name by working in Japan. He is the most modern out of these three which we are talking about here.

Dr Deming, Juran and Crosby. Crosby is the most modern quality guru. So if we look at the history of Phillip Crosby he started working in 1952 in the field of quality as a test technician in the quality department of Crosley Corporation and then in 1979 he started a management consulting company called Philip Crosby Associates

Incorporated and at the same time he published his book. This was his first business book called Quality is Free which really made him famous and he sold 1 million copies of that. This book basically emphasized that by investing in quality you get more return, so in a way getting quality or improving quality is free. That was the basic theme of this book that quality is free. You really don't need to spend more money to make a better quality product because you save in other ways. So that was the emphasis of the book which is Quality is Free. So this was the brief history of Philip Crosby.

Philip Crosby is best known for

So here in this chapter I have a brief list of achievements of Philip Crosby. He was a famous management consultant, moving around the globe, helping companies achieve quality. He did a lot of quality work. But what I'm listing here is just a very few of those things. One thing is his definition of quality. His definition of quality was that the quality is conforming to specification because his point was that you really cannot keep the definition of quality as vague. So when you say customer satisfaction, when you say the quality is fitness for use he was not in favor of that. He was in favor of having the definition of quality which is achievable, which is very specific that here is the specification.

If you achieve the specification you have achieved the quality. So that was his definition of quality. Then he gave four absolutes of quality. Those are very important teachings of Philip Crosby. We will go to each of these next few chapters and then in addition to that he published a number Of courses and the most famous out of these is free and quality without tears. If you are interested, go to Amazon and buy these books. These might not be very costly as compared to the Juran handbook. The latest copy of the Juran handbook might cost you $150. These books might cost you maybe around 10 to 20 dollars at the max. Go to Amazon, buy these books and study if you are really interested in making a career out of quality management.

Four Absolutes of Quality

So when we talked about the achievements of Philip Cosby. One of the items in that was four absolutes of quality. In this chapter I've just listed these four absolute items and in the next four chapters we will talk about each of these separately. But let's quickly go through that here and then we'll understand each of these as a separate item in a separate chapter. The first one is that the definition of quality is conformance to requirements. We have briefly talked about that. The second absolute quality is that the system of quality is prevention. So here the approach is prevention rather than being reactive. The third absolute quality is that the performance standard is zero defect. The aim should be to have zero defects. And the fourth absolute of quality is that the measurement of quality is the price of nonconformance. Next four chapters let's go through each of these four one by one.

Absolute #1: Quality is Conformance to Requirements

So let's look at the first absolute of quality provided by Philip Crosby and that is that the definition of Quality is Conformance to Requirements. Crosby was in favor of having a fixed definition of quality, something which you can achieve, something which is measurable. Quality doesn't mean something good, something elegant. You really can have a vague definition of quality if you really want to achieve quality. To achieve quality you need to have something which is achievable if you have a specification to tell workers to achieve the specification. That's quality. If you need to make a shaft which is 100 millimeters long, if 100 millimeters long, let's say plus minus 1 millimeter. If that's your specification.

If you achieve that it's quality. If you don't achieve that it's not quality. Let's not mix that with goodness. The client satisfaction and many other things because those are confusing things. You really cannot ask your task force, your team members or your workers to do something which makes the client happy that someone else's job is to put all those things as a part of specification. Once those are put as a specification. Ask your people. Ask your team. Ask a worker just to follow those instructions, just to follow those specifications. If you achieve that it's quality. Another thing which is emphasized in this point is that you do it right the first time. So you have a specification, achieved the specification requirement first time no rework.

And then in regards to management what Crosby asked was that management need to set those specifications, those requirements. So management is responsible for setting up those definitions of requirements, those specifications and people who are working are supposed to achieve that. That's the way you can achieve Quality

Consistently and then management needs to help people meet those requirements. So whatever help or whatever support, whatever tools, techniques people need, workers need management is responsible for providing those.

That's the second job of management and the third job of management proposed by Crosby is spending time helping employees meet those requirements. See where things can go wrong. See if there's additional support required. Management needs to get engaged and see that the workers are able to meet the requirements, so these are the three jobs related to management and workers are responsible to achieve specification. So that's how quality is defined.

Absolute #2: The System of Quality is Prevention

And the second absolute of quality proposed by Philip Crosby is that the System of Quality is Prevention, you achieve quality by prevention. In this Book we have talked about the cost of quality as well. In that we say that the cost of quality has three main components- prevention, appraisal and failure. But Crosby is in favor of putting more investment on prevention not on appraisal. Prevention is something whatever you do to make sure that the problems do not happen, you train people, you have the right tools and techniques. You have the right systems.

That's part of prevention, appraisal is testing, inspection. So rather than emphasizing on inspection and testing, put more emphasis on putting the systems in the right chapter people have the right to do. That's what this point emphasizes on is that the system of quality is prevention. You achieve quality by prevention. You invest well on prevention less on appraisal and failure costs. And what he said was that when you look at prevention, if you prevent something then error doesn't happen. Error doesn't happen, you really cannot miss that in the inspection. So if the error is not there in the piece itself, you really cannot miss when you inspect that.

And just like many other gurus his emphasis is on processes. Look at the processes rather than focusing on people. And the secret of prevention is to look at the process and identify the opportunities for error where things can go wrong. Look at those processes, improve those processes, once you improve the processes. Then there is less and less chance that the errors can happen. So this was the second absolute of quality provided by Philip Crosby which is that the System of Quality is Prevention.

Absolute #3: The Performance Standard is Zero Defects

The third absolute quality provided by Philip Crosby is that The Performance Standard is Zero Defect. And his point was the zero defect is not a motivational program, it is a management standard which tells people what management is expecting people from so the management is expecting zero defects. And for that management is responsible for looking at the processes, supporting processes, providing all the support people need. This might slightly contradict with the teachings of Dr. Deming. Dr Deming was not in favor of these approaches of zero defects putting a target but the philosophy is different. The thinking is different. Here Dr.

Crosby is looking for a zero defect as a program, as a management expectations and management working towards providing all the facilities, all the support, all the processes to achieve that rather than just plainly telling, putting a big poster that we are looking for zero defect. No, Crosby is not in favor of that. Crosby is in favor of having zero defects as the standard. That's what management should be expecting. And then management should be working to put all the systems and processes in place, all the resources which are required to achieve this standard which is a zero defect. Mistakes in any process are caused by two main factors.

One is the lack of knowledge. And second is lack of attention. So we need to tackle both of these. If a problem is happening because of a lack of knowledge then it's very simple. You need to provide that knowledge. You need to provide the processes, chapters, and all the support which a worker needs because if there's a lack of knowledge there will be a problem. So you need to overcome that. So this is one cause of making mistakes which is a lack of knowledge. The second cause of mistake is the lack of attention that's where workers or the people who are working on the job need to work on. It's an attitude problem.

So you need to understand that when you have a problem you need to understand what's the cause of that problem. Is it because of lack of knowledge, lack of resources, lack of attention, you find are the root cause of that. Work on that and look toward the zero defect as a basic standard of achieving quality. So this was the third absolute quality which is that The Performance Standard is Zero Defect, management needs to focus on having zero defect. You really cannot have a target of 1 percent repair. You really don't mean to have one percent product being made wrong. The standard should always be zero defects. So this is the third absolute quality provided by Philip Crosby.

Absolute #4: The Measurement of Quality is the Price of Non-

Coming to this fourth and the last absolute of quality proposed by Philip Crosby which is that The Measurement of Quality is the Price of Nonconformance. How do you measure quality, you measure quality by finding out the cost of quality. Cost of nonconformance, in the cost of quality chapters in this Book. We have talked about three types of major costs of quality. The prevention cost, appraisal cost and the failure cost. When we talk of prevention and appraisal those two costs are the price of conformance.

That's something that you pay to make sure that your product is right. So you pay to prevent something, you pay to appraise something, so these two aspects together form the price of conformance. The price of nonconformance is the failure cost. Failure could be internal, failure could be external. The key point Crosby wanted to emphasize here was that the management understands the language of money. The dollar value, you need to put the quality in the form of those dollar values, numbers in terms of the price of conformance, numbers in terms of price of non-conformance.

If you put those numbers you will be able to convince your management to invest in the processes, to invest in new machinery, to invest in whatever is required to achieve quality. If you put these numbers in terms of dollar value that can really help in making management quick decisions on these things. So this was the fourth absolute of quality proposed by Philip Crosby which is that the measurement of quality is the price of non-conformance.

So with this we completed the discussion on four absolutes provided by Phillip Crosby. There are lots and lots of teaching provided by Phillip Crosby. If you are really interested you can look at the literature, go

through the works, buy his books which is let's say Quality is Free, Quality without Tears. Read those things you will learn more about Philip Crosby. But the intent here was just to give you a brief overview of these three quality gurus- Dr Deming, Dr. Juran and Philip Crosby.

Practice Activity - Quiz - Quality Gurus

So far in this Book we have looked at some basic aspects related to quality. We have looked at various definitions of quality. They looked at Garvin's eight dimensions of quality, understood the difference between QA QC ,looked at the history of quality and we have also looked at the work of three major quality gurus. Your question would be what about my current job. Where do I fit this quality knowledge into my current work? Quality cost is one of the important aspects to raise the awareness of quality.

So whatever work you are doing, look at the cost of quality that will give you a good idea where you stand. And when I say cost of quality there are two aspects of cost of quality. One is something which you can see which is visible and then the second aspect of that is something which is not visible or which is invisible and then the cost of quality can be segregated into number of buckets, number of categories. On the right side of this chapter I have 4 major categories of quality cost- Prevention, Appraisal, Internal failure, External failure.

Once you look at all these things in regards to your current job that will really give you a good understanding where you stand in regards to quality. The concept of quality cost was introduced way back in 1956 by quality guru Feigen baum. He wrote an article in Harvard Business Review at that time that is the foundation of this concept of cost of quality. Let's get to the next chapter and learn about two parts of the cost of quality, one which is visible and one which is not visible. And then we even look into these four categories. So let's move to the next chapter and look at the difference between the visible cost of quality and the visible cost of quality.

Visible vs Invisible Cost of Poor Quality

Whenever you talk about cost of quality the first thing which comes to your mind is the rejection. If you make something wrong then you need to reject that or you might need to rework that, repair that. The cost of the inspection, these are the types of things which come to your mind in the first instance that whenever things go wrong this is where you will be paying for that wrongdoing, paying in form of rejection. paying in the form of rework, repair or the cost of reinspection. But if you look at deeper into the cost of quality there are a number of aspects which you really don't see.

The cost of quality is the sail loss which occurs because your client is not satisfied with the quality which you are producing. So today if you are selling 100 pieces a day, quality goes down, you lose your customers, you lose your sale and maybe during the next period you will be selling 50 pieces instead of hundred pieces, so that's a lost sale. Another Invisible aspect is excess inventory. So if you don't sell those items which you produced then that will lead to the extra inventory in your place and extra inventory basically means that there is a cost tied to that. The cost of production, the cost of raw material, all those things now are lying in your own store because you are not able to sell that. So that's another cost of poor quality. Let's look at a few more here which are additional controls and procedures.

So if your quality is poor then you need to put some extra checkpoints, extra hole points, extra procedures to make sure that you produce things right. There will be complaints. You need to handle those customer complaints, you need to do some investigation. Probably if something really goes wrong then you really need to do a good investigation to find out the root cause of that problem. There could be fines related to some problems which have been happening in the hands of your client. There could be a legal fee. Lots and lots of costs of poor quality which you probably don't realize in the first instance, in the first instance you just think that the cost of quality means rejection, repair, rework. But then there is a lot of hidden cost of quality.

Classification - Cost of Conformance and Non-conformance

We can classify the cost of quality into three broad categories. One is t Prevention. Whatever cost we are occurring to prevent things from going wrong. That's a prevention cost. The next will be Appraisal, appraisal is the cost of maintaining the quality by uprising by checking by inspecting. And the third cost of quality is Failure. If everything fails then there is a cost related to the failure that becomes the failure cost of quality. In failure also there are two aspects whether that failure has occurred Internally or Externally. So if that has occurred internally what you do then in that case would be you will repair, reject or whatever you do.

But if that happens externally, externally in the hands of the customer then there are costs related to that. We will be looking at these let's say four categories- Prevention, Appraisal, Internal Failure and External failure in next four chapters and understand what these costs constitute of. What is included in prevention cost, what is included in the appraisal cost of quality, what is included in internal failure and external failure cost of quality. Let's see that in the next four chapters.

Cost of Quality - 1. Prevention Cost

So as we earlier said that the Prevention Cost is all those costs which are spent to avoid the nonconformists, to avoid the poor quality. This is something which you invest beforehand as a proactive measure to avoid the quality problems. And the costs related to that would be considered as prevention cost. Prevention costs could include quality planning. So whatever planning you are doing to make sure that you make the right thing the first time, that will be the cost of prevention. Whatever money you are spending on education and chapter to avoid any problems, that's the prevention cost. Any designed review which you do beforehand to avoid the quality problem happening in the first place will be considered as prevention cost. There could be a number of prevention costs.

So as I'm going through these four costs of quality- Prevention, Appraisal, Internal failure and External failure. I would suggest that you take a piece of paper and pen and write it down in your work area. What type of costs you are incurring as prevention cost. What cost you are incurring an appraisal, Internal failure or External failure. Look at that from your own product or service point of view. Here I'm just giving you a few high level examples of each of these costs. So we talked about the prevention cost here. Let's move onto the next chapter and look at the appraisal cost of quality.

Cost of Quality - 2. Appraisal Cost

So the Prevention Cost which we talked about earlier was related to preventing the problems happening in the first place. The next one here is the Appraisal Cost, Appraisal Cost is for maintaining the quality level. Whatever checks and balances we have in our process to make sure that we maintain the quality, those will be considered as the appraisal cost. Appraisal Cost will consist of tests and inspection, whatever checking you're doing in process, whatever checking you're doing as a final product all will be included as the cost of appraisal. In addition to that when you buy some material from your suppliers the suppliers sampling whatever testing you're doing on those items which you purchased that also will be considered as the appraisal cost. So the appraisal cost will also include auditing processes whatever you do to maintain the quality level whatever you have.

Some of the auditing Of course might be considered as the prevention cost if you're doing an audit of your supplier for selecting that supplier. That's something which I would say that you're doing something for prevention rather than appraisal. Appraisal will be once you have a supplier in place and you are doing an audit on that particular supplier to make sure that the supplier is able to provide you the consistent product that would be considered as appraisal. So an audit could basically fall in any of these two categories depending upon the purpose of that audit. And both of these prevention and appraisal are basically targeting to eliminate or reduce the internal and external failure costs.

Cost of Quality - 3. Internal Failure Cost

The next category of the cost of quality is the Internal Failure Cost. Internal failure cost is related to all the failures which happen within the organization before it leaves the boundary of the organization or before it reaches the hands of the customer. In internal failure cost we could consider the in-process scrapping and re- working. So if your process has produced something wrong you scrap that, you reject that or you do the work to make it right. The cost incurred in that would be the internal failure cost, any trouble shooting or repairing which you're doing that's the internal failure cost. Any design changes you make based on the problems you are facing would be internal failure cost.

Then you have problems then you need to keep extra inventory, extra inventory to make sure that your production continues. So for example if your target is to produce 100 pieces but then you know that 10 pieces every 100 pieces might have a problem. So you need to keep those ten pieces extra. So instead of targeting 100 pieces you'll be targeting one hundred and ten pieces with the assumption that 10 might have some problems as we go further. So that extra inventory the money which ties up in extra inventory those ten pieces which we were talking about would be considered as the cost of quality because to maintain the inventory you need to spend money and then you will need some space to keep those extra pieces, you will need some extra handling.

So all these costs basically will add up and give you a big number once you look at that cost. So if you have reworked some items, so the item was wrong you corrected that but then you need to spend extra money on the inspecting, rechecking that item which you corrected. So there is extra money involved in retesting as well. And many times you cannot bring that repaired product to that top level quality whatever you are producing, whatever you're giving to the customer. But then in that case you will downgrade that product and sell that cheaper to some other customers. So the amount which you get less because of downgrading that also will be considered as the cost of quality.

So now if you look at these numbers, these numbers are huge and the cost of internal and external failure is basically a big amount. Internal would be still less but external could mean a lot. Any external failure might really cost you a lot of money. So whatever money you can spend in preventing as a first attempt, uprising as a second layer of production and then maybe the last layer of production is internal failure because even at internal failure also you are good because you got that problem before it reaches the hands of the customer. But once it goes out the cost implications might be huge. Let's look at those costs which are related to external failure in the next chapter.

Cost of Quality - 4. External Failure Cost

In this classification of cost of quality the last item here is External Failure. This is something that you need to avoid at any cost whatever you do, whatever money you spent in the top three it's still worth rather than going through this amount of money which will be spent in External Failure. When it comes to external failure let's look at some examples of those. Examples could be sales, returns and allowances whatever returns you get because of repairs and rejection. Those would be considered as the external failure cost. And if you have a service level agreement the penalties because of that would be the external failure cost. For example my website host gives me a warranty that my website will be up and running for ninety nine point ninety nine percent of time.

But if that company fails to maintain that service level agreement there's a penalty involved related to that and the cost of that would be considered as the external failure cost. External failure cost will include complaints handling, whatever complaints you are getting from your customers handling those, managing those the department which you have set up for all that cost is related to external failure cost. Because if your product was good you could have avoided all these costs related to complaint handling. **** Another example here could be the field service labor and parts costs because you have some warranty obligation.

So you need to send your technician to get that thing repaired. That's a cost related to external failure cost, much bigger than these costs would be the cost of a recall. You would have heard a number of cases related to recall where because of the problem the company had to recall their products back. Whether that's Toyota, Toyota has gone to a big recall. A number of other companies have gone through big recalls which have cost them maybe millions, maybe billions of dollars for handling those complaints, handling those quality issues. And then there could be some legal claims lawsuits which you have to fight because of the problem because of the quality issues which were in the product.

So these costs really could be very big and could really affect the company as a whole. So whatever you want to do you look at these four costs and see how much you're spending in these categories and where you can spend more. Many a times it's not really practical to maintain all these costs, this many a times still remains a theoretical concept but it gives a very strong indication that you need to avoid internal and external costs. If you spend a little bit more on prevention, a little bit more on appraisal it is still worth doing that because that way you can avoid the big cost which could be related to internal or external failures.

Number of times people have a question about how much percent of cost should be in each of these categories. How much money we should be spending on prevention. How much money we should be spending on appraisal. There is no direct answer to that because it all depends from industry to industry. The company and the company and many times as I said earlier that might not be a very good accounting mechanism to maintain all these costs.

But the point here is that each employee in the organization should understand that there are costs related to these four categories and they need to understand that any attempt to avoid internal and external failure costs will be good for the organization. Management needs to understand that they need to spend more money in prevention and some money in appraisal rather than spending lots and lots of money on Internal and External Failure. So these were four categories of costs of quality. In the next chapter very quickly look at why we need this.

Why to Measure the Cost of Quality?

So the question here is why do we need to measure the cost of quality. And as I earlier said that it's not a very easy thing to classify these costs into these four categories and maintain that it's not easy. There is no common accounting standard for these things but these things still can be maintained at a high level. Any external cost, any major cost you can really maintain and see where you are spending more.

The reason to do that would be the first thing is that management understands the language of money. So management really might not be interested in the very detailed parts of each of these quality aspects but management would always be interested in knowing about money. Management would be interested in seeing how we avoid cost. How do we make money? So you can make money by avoiding all those big failures which could happen internally or externally.

And for that as a quality professional or as employee you have a justification that the money spent on improving or preventing activities is still a good investment because that investment can help you in reducing those failure costs and you might want to use these cost to set the target to reduce your cost, to reduce costs related to internal and external failure by investing more in appraisal and prevention. So this completes our discussion on the Cost of Quality. No we understand the cost of quality but as an individual employee how can we help in reducing the cost of quality.

One aspect of that would be reducing wastes and when I talk of reducing wastes let's understand that Toyota as a company which is pioneer in quality management, they introduce the concept of lean management. And in that seven or eight types of wastes are defined. So if each employee understands these types of wastes what can happen in your own work process they can definitely help in reducing those wastes.

So any employee in the organization needs to understand where all wastes are happening in their own work processes because that understanding can really help in driving down the cost, driving down the cost of quality. So with this basic understanding let's move on to the next chapter and look at the types of wastes because that can really help us in reducing the cost.

Benefits Of Effective Time Management

Hi Everybody! This is Professor and welcome to the Advanced Ideas chapter of "Ultimate Time Management." This could easily be the most important chapter you do all year ... for many people in their entire life. So, let's look at some of the goals of the chapter. Now, the first one is the Time Management Program. We want to save you a ton of time, not a little bit of time, not a few extra minutes a day, a ton of time, sometimes years of your life. Second thing, is we want to help you move your career along faster. It doesn't have to be so slow. We can move you ahead years faster and we'll prove it to you. 3) We're going to improve the productivity of your staff. If you have people working under you, maybe this is your own business. This will help move your career along faster.

Help save you problems, make your unit more productive. And if you own the company, it's going to put a lot of money in your pocket. If you don't own the company, it's going to make you look good. Get those promotions and put more money in your pocket. And that's our next thing is to help you get what? More money in your pocket. Did I mention money in your pocket enough? I hope I did. Because this is going to do it in a lot of different ways. Saving time and saving money are the same things. Some of these time savers are actually going to show you ways to make more money while you're saving time. So four is not a duplicate, It's just to stress how many different ways we're going to help you out in this chapter. Number five, and this is not a small one, to reduce your stress. Here's my definition of stress.

I give you a 20 hour project and I give you eight hours to do it. We call that massive stress. Here's stress reduction. I give you an eight hour project and I give you 20 hours to do it. That's called "Massive Relaxation." When you learn to save time, The way we're talking about in this chapter about saving time, your stress is going to go down significantly, because it's going to give you so much time back. Make you, your team, your processes, so much more productive ... that your stress is going to crash. Perfect! 6) We want to give you years of your life back, not a couple of minutes. I didn't say minutes, I didn't say hours, I didn't say days, I didn't say months, YEARS of your life back. And some people, because of some of the techniques we're showing you here, they couldn't have accomplished what they accomplished, in their entire lifetime without these strategies.

So maybe, for those people, we gave him their entire life back. Not bad right? Now, the first thing I want to give you is a definition of Time Management. I define it as "Regaining Control of your Time and your Life." Now, here's why I specify time and life, because time and life are the SAME thing. The first thing I want you to understand is that time and life are the SAME thing! There is no difference. Here's a great quote, you should write this down. Print out this chapter. Put it up on your wall. "Life is naught but a measurement of time. You cannot waste one without losing the other." So our life and our time are of ultimate importance. Hold in mind that your life is your greatest asset. Bar none. Never forget that you can't bank time. You say, "Well, maybe I'll take an hour from today and I'll spend it tomorrow." Absolutely NO such thing.

"Use it or lose" is the policy that's currently in effect. Next, People who waste your time are STEALING your life. Remember time and life are the same thing. These people aren't stealing your time, they're stealing your life, they're killing you! Next, Are people helping you SPEND your time or WASTE your time? When I was a kid I used to say, "I'll go out with my buddy and blow a couple of hours at the ballpark or do whatever." Blow a couple hours? Blow your life? Blow your time? Blow your whole life away? NO! When you spend your time, and remember time is money, right? So time has a monetary value. You better be getting something that is of equal or greater value. Say, you think your time is worth it, maybe you make 40,000 a year.

You think your time is just worth 20 bucks an hour. Did you spend your hour on something that was worth at least 20 bucks? So any time you spend an hour, was it worth at least 20 bucks? Now, if you want to start making 300 bucks an hour, if you want to start making that kind of money, don't do any activity that wouldn't pay 300 bucks an hour. Start doing higher level activities. Obviously, you won't start there, but I want you in your mind to start ticking up the value of your time. Then, you're either going to end up with more time or more money. If you do it correctly according to all the parameters we're going to teach you here, you'll have both. So always be thinking, are people helping you spend your time or waste your time? And finally, always be searching for new ways to save time.

This Book is a Beginning ... It's not the end. It has some of the greatest time management tips and techniques and values out there. It does not have all of them. And finally, for this chapter, I leave you with this thought. It's from a great book by Ogmund Mandino. It says, "What rich man, old and sick, feeble and helpless, would not exchange all the gold in his vault for the blessings you have treated so lightly." What blessings are we talking about? We're talking about time. Right now. You've got Bill Gates and he's worth over a hundred billion dollars, that's a hundred thousand million dollars. A hundred thousand million dollars, you can't even imagine that much money! Do you think he'd hand you a billion dollars right now if he were on his deathbed and you could give him just one more day? Yeah, matter of fact, he might even empty out his whole—vault! I'm sure he leaves some money aside for his kids ... But yeah, you would see a good chunk of that. That's how valuable your time is, once you start to value your time. You are doing fantastic. I'll see you in the next chapter.

3 Main Concepts For Effective Time Management

Welcome back everybody. So, what are our goals? Save time, save money. Now, we said that your life and your time are the same thing, time and money are the same thing as well. Keep those two in mind. Now we're going to jump into the core principles. The three fundamentals of time management. Make sure these three are going OK, and then we'll be prepared to jump into the next chapter, which is the specific techniques of Time Management. Now, here's a great quote by Stephen Covey. It says, "What if you get to the top of the ladder, only to find it's leaning against the wrong wall?" What does it mean? Well, you try to get from point A to Point B. You're trying to accomplish your goal in life. What if you picked the wrong model? What if you picked the wrong goal? What if you went in, you got a four year degree in psychology and you really want to be a medical doctor. Psychology they do from the neck up, medical doctors they do from the neck down.

You were close, but you've missed it. It would be a massive fail, wildly expensive, 12 years out of your life. Boom! Starting over from square one. Massive losses. And you feel stupid. You've got to spend some time planning! There's no sense going in the wrong direction at a high rate of speed, make sense? Make sure you do this. Otherwise, you're wasting years of your life. Here's your next concept. Always start with the end in mind. Now, you used to start at point "A". You want to get Point "B" and you simply did every step in between. So the old mindset was that "The shortest distance between two points is a straight line." No. The new thinking, the improved thinking, not the gold level of thinking, but the platinum level of thinking, is that the shortest distance between two points is a RESOURCE.

See the old thinking was the shortest "distance." Say, I take a letter and I write something down and I lick it, and I stick it, and I dutifully put it in the mail. Mailman walks directly to his car, and doesn't waste any time. Takes his car, drives it to the post office, puts it in another car, and goes to the airport. They fly directly to the next site. They take a truck and they go directly from point A to Point B. They go directly to the nearest post office, the nearest post office hands it to the mailman, they drive directly to your house and they drop it off. That is the shortest distance between two points. Now, we can do it almost like it's Star Trek and we can teleport, right? We do email. Email is a RESOURCE. It's NOT the shortest distance between two points. A resource is the shortest distance between two points. You can do this a lot of different ways, you can do this with technology, you can do this with networking, you can do it with consulting. There's a lot of different ways to get from point A to Point B ... Besides going in a straight line. So hold that idea. Think about that idea. Remember that idea.

Now, here's one of the greatest principals in all of time management. This is called the "Pareto Principle." This was started by Vilfredo Pareto. You can't make this stuff up. Vilfredo Pareto, appropriate name, kind of sounds Italian, right? He was an Italian economist and what he did was, he was studying land rights. He wanted to see what was going on with land rights in Italy and he noticed that 20 percent of the population owned about 80 percent of the land. The other 80 percent of the population owned the remaining 20 percent. So, he created something called the "Pareto Principle" when he wondered if this kind of formula worked for other things. Now, they call it the 80:20 rule, but it's not always exactly 80/20 ... might be 70/30, 90/10, 75/25 ... but it floats around 80/20. So, what is the "Pareto Principle" and/or also known as, AKA, "The 80/20 Rule." Well, it works in two directions.

Say, 20 percent of your clients equal 80 percent of your sales. That's true. There are also another 20 percent of your clients that equal 80 percent of your problems. (LOL) Those are probably the 20 percent you want to get rid of, Right? So, 20 percent of what you do on any given day, remember this, 20 percent of what you do, equals 80 percent of the value. Look at it. Everything you do. What do I actually get paid for? What are my highest value tasks? ... and always start with those. If you could only get one of these done, would you want to get the 20 percent done? That's worth 80 percent of the value? or would you want to get the 80 percent done, that's worth 20 percent of the value? You want to get the 20 percent done that's worth 80 percent of that money! That's right! Because, it's a quarter of the work and it's worth four times as much.

Beautiful. So, principle number one, know what the 80 percent is. Know what the 20 percent is. Step 2, always get the 20 percent done! Make sure it gets done. I would go by making it, get done first. Now, here's what we want to do. Figure out that 20 percent of what you're doing that makes 80 percent of the money, this is step three. I want you to see how much of that 80 percent that only makes 20 percent of the money you can eliminate ... and how much of that 20 percent that makes the 80 percent of the money you can duplicate. If you do this, and you're really effective, you should get that 20 percent to take up 80 percent of your time and there's going to be 20 percent left that just can't be eliminated. But by the time you do that much, you will be making four times as much money, for no more additional effort. Hear that? Four times as much money for NO more additional effort! Learn, understand, worship at the altar of the Pareto Principle. A major key timesaver.

Specific Time Management Techniques 1

Ladies and gentlemen, the moment we've all been waiting for ... "Specific Time Management Techniques." Specific Management Technique number one, Voice Recognition Software. I like to brag that I can do a hot 25 words per minute hunt and peck, you know the old two finger typist. That's actually pretty good for two fingers. Voice recognition will now do 80 to 125 words per minute. This is realistic. This is not what they list on the box and all that type of stuff, they'll tell you, they can do 150 to 200 words per minute. No. After you've made any corrections, you're slowing down, you're pronouncing your words correctly. Any corrections that you've got to make, about 80 to one 125 words per minute.

So now it's a significant jump. Back in the day, you had to buy a really nice program like Dragon Naturally Speaking. When I got my first computer, the dream was that I would get this really high speed computer ... it was probably going 150 megahertz at the time. Now they're all gigahertz, but that I'd be able to talk into my computer and it would be able to type it out for me. And I was doing a fast hunt and pecking at about 25 words per minute and when I spoke it would do between 15 and 20 words per minute ... It was really disappointing. So, the technology wasn't where it needed to be back in the 90s. Obviously, this isn't the 90s anymore. The technology was largely slowed down, like I said, mine was a megahertz, it was the speed of the computer and the RAM.

Because voice recognition takes up a huge amount of memory. So, voice recognition can get you typing about four times as fast. And what's nice is, at least windows to date has always given a FREE voice recognition software. That's about as good as you can buy on the market even if you buy Dragon Naturally Speaking, which I love. I use that all the time.

That's about $100 to $400 software, depending on which version you buy. But the Windows version works about 98 percent as good as that, and it's FREE! So, I would go with that one before I try any other one. At least use it for comparison. Voice recognition can save you a ton of time and for a lot of people, speaking things out is easier in their train of thought than talking things out.

So, absolute gold. Make sure you get this. Next, I call my "Traveling University" and my "University on wheels." One of the ways I got a huge education and a huge jump on everybody else and saved a boatload of time in doing it, was my university on wheels and my traveling university. I always had some kind of literature that would travel with me, it could be a book I put underneath my arm, if I didn't want to carry around the book, I used to photocopy some pages and stick them in my back pocket. So, I used to call it the "Butt Technique", wherever I went my butt was nearby. (LOL) It was within arm's reach, right? So, even if I forgot the book and I forgot the CD, and I didn't have my MP 3 player, now you can download everything onto your phone.

I used to use a PDA. I mean, you have to have a laptop, which used to have a bulky CD player. Now, things are so much better. Technology is getting better and better and better. So, your Traveling University can be CDs and MP3s books, magazines, saved articles that you copy. Like I said you photocopy it can be put in your back pocket. I love Kindle, Kindle, Kindle, Kindle. Because I can always, anytime I've got nothing to do, I get something to do. I can read a Kindle book on my cell phone. Now I can highlight it, take notes and everything else they're, really advanced now. I always keep a flash drive with me with some extra materials.

I have a flash drive that I plug into my car that plays the MP3s. There's a lot of different ways to do it today. A lot of people just play their media out through their cell phone and that'll even project out through the car. So, technology is getting really great about allowing us to use our downtime. So, driving, the average commute is 20 minutes each way, that's 40 minutes per day, you could be learning something. If you just do that five days a week, take the weekends off, and you do that for a year, that's worth half a semester of college or half a year of college. So, one semester or half a year at college. So, every eight years you get a four year degree. Nice. If you listen a little bit more, do it when you are walking the dog, mowing the lawn, going out for a walk, any time you have downtime.

You could easily get a year or more of education while you're doing nothing. I do it when I'm waiting for meetings, whenever I get five minutes together. When I'm waiting for doctor's office, dentist, I don't care if he's waiting in line at Wal-Mart. I don't know why, I think they have a magical thing where if there's less than six people in line, they find some way to slow it down. So, this is one of the things that any time you get nothing to do, you get something to do. I want you to hear a ticking clock in the background as you go through time management saying tick, tick, tick. I'm going to translate tick, tick, tick, tick, from tick to English, tick tick tick means "I'm losing money, I'm losing money, I'm losing money, I'm losing money, I'm losing money."

Here's the other thing. "Somebody is getting ahead of me. Somebody is getting ahead of me. Somebody is getting ahead of me. Somebody is getting ahead of me." Hear that in your head and you won't waste your time. Next technique, and everybody should nail this down. Learn it as early in your career as you can, teach it to your kids ... Learn Speed Reading! There's an old quote that says, "Readers are Leaders." Why? Because the smartest guy gets the job. Despite what a lot of the line people think. Let me tell you what the fastest way to speed read is, look at the cover. You really CAN judge a book by the cover. Barnes and

Noble actually did a study and said, 90 percent of people who buy their books, they only looked at the cover.

They never looked inside. So, fastest way to speed read, look at the cover, read the inside of the book jacket, just the front part which tells you what the book's about and at the back part which tells you about the author, that's what I call the "I Love Me" chapter, read through the table of contents and then flip through the table contents. Find your favorite chapter and read a paragraph or two to see if you like their style and if they immediately give you value. If they're not, the average book takes about 20 hours to read. So I'm teaching you the fastest way to speed read. Do just what I told you. It'll take you under two minutes and then slam the book down and say, "Oh my god, this is the worst piece of junk I ever seen ..." and save yourself 20 hours.

That's the fastest way to speed read! (LOL) Now, there's other ways to speed read ... You can follow your finger and read the text. Do you know if you follow your finger and read the text and you do that for about 15 to 20 minutes. After about day three or four or five, somewhere in there, you're going to start reading 25 percent faster! Which means in the time that somebody else can read four books, you can read a fifth one, maybe a little more. That's awesome! So, one of the things that I want to do, is don't use that as your speed reading Book, but that's a couple of different ways to speed read. I want you to take a speed reading Book. Spend the money. And on average, people get at least double the reading speed with the same or higher comprehension.

And people really practice it the way you should practice it can go about four to five times faster. Awesome! Huge time saver. Web surfing, HUGE time waster! Several studies have shown that web surfing on average, wastes one to three hours per day. That's a huge amount of time. And it's much closer to the three, it's skewed over to that area. If you were to time yourself, and we call it quote, unquote, web surfing, add in all your cell phone time which is your portable web, ... and you'll find it might be five or six hours a day. It just gets huge fast! Say you came out around two hours a day. Every four years. That's one full year of labor. So figure out how much you make in a year ... and in four years, that's how much I waste every four years.

You could, if you spent that same amount of time working, you'd be able to retire about 10 years early with about five times as much money as anybody else. It's a huge amount of time to waste and money to waste. It's a killer of time! And I've done this in seminars, I have like 300 people in the room and I'll say, "Hey, how many people like to surf the web?" All these hands go up, "Hey, how many people like to play with your cell phones?" Oh yeah, I love to do that, I love to watch stuff on my cell phone. I say, "How many people spend an hour a day." Bunch of hands go up. "How many people spend 2 hours a day doing that?" Bunch of hands go up. "How many people spend 3 hours a day?" Bunch of hands go up. "How many people spend 4 hours a day?" Bunch of hands go up.

Five, six, seven, bunch of hands start going down, OK. But a huge amount of people spend that much time on their cell phone or the web. Then I do a final thing, I say, "Show of hands, how many of you have earned even $1 surfing the web or using your cell phone?" Very few hands go up, maybe two or three, like less than 1% out of 100. The rest we're all just WASTING their time. These are people that didn't have time to get a college degree. These are people that don't have time to work overtime. These are people that don't have time to get a promotion, to go to chapter, to spend time with their kids, to spend time with their families, to take time off, and they waste all this time web surfing, and messing with their cell phone.

Don't let it be you. Look at those people like that, like a fool. If I'm on the web, it's because I'm doing a chapter, It's because I'm gathering some information, it's because I'm downloading a resource, I'm working on something, like building up my social media. Why? To sell to those people. Don't waste time. That's one of the biggest time wasters. If you can just get that time back, your life will be transformed. Now, your final tip for this chapter. I'm going to kind of tell you the opposite. Go ahead and use that cell phone. (LOL) There's some great productivity apps. Certain apps that are on there, they can save you a ton of time. Sorry, "Clash of Clans"is not one of them. "Angry Birds" is not one of them. Don't be playing games there. Don't do social media. Leave that alone! But, Great Productivity Apps, Audio Recorders, Note Takers, Calendars, Microsoft Word, Kindle books, Audio books, all kinds of productivity apps.

There's a productivity app for almost anything that could be saving you time. So look through the apps and see which ones are saving time, which ones are losing time, and you'll know what to do. Just like any good manager. People that are losing you money, fire them, people that are making you money, hire them, Ok? And go through your apps like that. And start looking for new apps. What are apps that could help me do everyday tasks that I didn't even think there was an app for? Go out, find it, get it, and I'll see you in the next chapter.

Specific Time Management Techniques 2

Here's a great tip that's going to save you money and time. Cancel your subscriptions! I'm telling you, if you haven't got time for the good stuff, skip the trash! Look at all these newspapers. I had a friend, he used to brag that every Sunday, he read the Sunday Times from cover to cover. Now, first of all he couldn't do that, because it takes about six days. AND that's a horrible thing to brag about! Why? Because most of it is bad news, all the news is bad. My favorite joke when I see somebody reading a newspaper is, "Any good news?" and they laugh and say," No, not today, not ever!" That's the reply, but the reply is sincere and it's honest and the joke is only funny because reading a newspaper, thinking you can find something good ... is a joke! Matter of fact, when I got out of college, I started reading The Wall Street Journal. I thought that made me smart.

But I was very targeted, even though I didn't read the Wall Street Journal from cover to cover. Where do I go? I went to the front page where all the major news is. In one page I got all the information. I went to the Money chapter, to look to see where to invest. I went to the back chapter, to see how my current investments were doing. Then I went to the health and technology chapter, so I could actually learn something, and I threw out the rest of the paper. Now, you might look at that and say, you threw out 90 percent of the paper! Yeah, I "Skipped the Trash." So even if there is a good magazine, a good newspaper that you're going to read, and don't get me wrong, you can find some tidbits in these.

Remember the Pareto Principle? 20 percent of what's in there is going to be worth 80 percent of the value. I think about 5 percent of what's in there is worth 95 percent of the value. So be very selective! And get rid of all the rubbish, especially stuff like People Magazine and all these InTouch Magazines and Miss Magazine. And all the rubbish ones that are just busy with other people's business. Until you get your life 100 percent squared away, don't start working on the Kardashian's life, don't start working on the local superstar, or football player's life. Don't worry about what they're doing. Worry about how MY life is going. Am I saving my time? So, use a time management perspective whenever you're going through any of these newspapers, any of these magazines, any of these subscriptions.

So one, skip the trash that will save you a bunch of time. Go ahead and cancel any subscriptions that you don't need because they are trash. And even if you're reading them, find the 5 percent which is the 90 percent ... Throw out the rest. Use that time wisely and enjoy it. Now, this is one of the biggest time management tips, EVER! Think of it this way, when you have a mentor, they might have been out in the field 10 years, 20 years, 30 years, 40 years, 50 years. They are going to take years off your learning curve. They're going to tell you in minutes or hours what took them years and decades. That is a HUGE savings! Also , they are going to save you a ton of costly errors. In A.A. they have an old expression, "Let me have done that for you" ... which means instead of using your brilliant plan to do blah, blah, blah ... I've already done it.

I can tell you how it comes out. Let me have done that for you ... and don't bother. Don't lose the wife, don't lose the job, don't go to jail. I already did that for you. I know what happens when you do A you get B. Let me tell you how it works out. That's what a mentor will do for you out there in the business world or the health world or whatever type of mentor you have. They will have already spent their money and their time, and their pain, to get you the valuable information. I can tell you as a therapist and an educator, there are two ways to learn. 1) Painful personal experience, also known as trial and error. Very, very painful, very costly in time, money, stress, in a lot of ways, 2) Then there's observational learning. Watch what this person does.

When they do something wrong, make a note of it and don't do that. When they do something right, make a note of that and do that over and over, and over again. A mentor is Observational Learning. It's education at its finest, at its most efficient and its most valuable. Next, the mentor is a huge store of valuable information. I had a buddy Nick. He had multiple degrees in everything and he says, " I hardly know anything. I know like one, one billionth of what there is to know out there." So, he says, "If I can't figure something out on my own with my vast store of knowledge in the first five to 10 minutes, I'm on the phone. I won't even strain my brain to try to figure it out. I'm not going to go through trial and error. I don't have to know everything." Listen to what he said. Write this down. "I just have to know who to ask." REPEAT: "I don't have to know everything.

I just have to know who to ask." That's a mentor! So, they're going to provide you with a lot of direction, they're going to provide you with a lot of support, they're going to help to encourage you. You can use them to bounce your ideas off of, get some feedback on them. A lot of times we don't want to tell people our brilliant ideas. You know why? One, sometimes people are discouraging when they should be encouraging. Other times, it's us. We know if we mention it to somebody, they'll immediately start picking out the flaws and we don't have a really good comeback. Which means we're hoping we're going to get lucky, when we really need to re-evaluate our plan. And that's where the mentor will stop you very gently and tell you, "Hey, good plan ... but I think we need to tweak these couple of areas, then it will be an excellent plan with an excellent chance of success." Now, the next area that they can help you with, is they can help you get connected with their network. Remember my buddy Nick said, "I don't know everything, I just have to know who to ask"? When you're first starting out, even when you've been out there for years, each person you add to your network has a network themselves.

So the first and best network, before I ever had a network ... was my buddy Nick. He knew a bunch of people, I didn't know anybody that had any valuable resources. Your mentor can help get you connected. And that brings us to the next part, which is Networking. MUCH of your success in life is truly going to be based on who you know. And what's that? That's your Network! So it doesn't mean, hey, I know this person, they're going to get me a job, that's the classic thing, so kind of nepotism or favoritism, or something, No. It simply means that we are successful in life, in almost direct one to one proportion to the number of people that know us, like us and trust us. That's our network.

Networking can get you ahead faster than anything. In life, We don't compete, We conspire, We work together. Fools compete ... They have egos. The people that are really going to get wealthy, they conspire, they work with everybody, ok. They want to make it happen, they want to create as many win- win situations and good connections as they can, and just make a lot of money together. Sometimes they don't trust somebody, but they trust their Greed and they can still network with them. This doesn't mean network with everybody, there's some people you want to avoid. But there are a ton of great people out there who can be life-changing.

This is one of the areas, the mentor and the networking, so two of the areas that can take years and even a lifetime off your work. There are some people that you can mentor with or can network with that will transform your life. I remember when I first started Internet marketing, I was working away, working away, working away. I finally found the great secret of how to make money online. I then shared it with some friends. They made a bunch of money online and boom. Why did they make all that money? Because they connected with me. It was life changing, they just happened to be in my network. I proposed this to them, and I only proposed it to three people, because those were the people that I knew, I liked and I trusted. I wanted to see them get ahead. I had one friend that was in bankruptcy.

This saved his house, his life, his marriage, everything! Boom! It put him back on track and put him in the green and gave him future income. This was everything to him. So, everything that he had made in his lifetime, he had lost .... and now he's recouped it. Why? He could have never done that on his own. He had success once. It wasn't really something that he could duplicate. And he was out there in the wind. But, because he had a good network. Boom! He's back in the money, So, when you're looking at networking, remember your life, your success will be a direct one to one proportion, write this down, direct one to one proportion to how many people know you, like you and trust you, So get out there and get networking.

The key to networking is to get good quality, so, always look at the quality. Look at the quantity, the number, quantity is NOT as important as quality. You want good quality contacts. As a matter of fact, if it's not good quality, I don't want them in there as part of my what? Does my quantity make sense? Skills, look for skills across a wide area and make sure you've covered what I call "Your Wheel". You need somebody that's good with health, you need somebody that's good with wealth, you need somebody who is good with finances, like an accountant, so, it's a little different than wealth. You need somebody that's good with therapy, like myself. a good therapist to check things out psychologically. You might need somebody that's good with physical fitness or whatever. So, might be spirituality for you, have people that have different Skills in all the major life areas. Don't leave a hole there.

Look for people to have influence ... that can get use zoning permits when you need it, That can get you pushed to the front of the line in different areas. You know what influences are. Finances are also important too. These are people that can loan you money or get you better rates or tell you where there's financial help available. I remember my business one of the biggest problems was just getting enough money together so I could make more money. I basically had an online machine to make money and I just needed some loans to make the money. Matter of fact, I was paying the loans off every single month. That's how much money I was making. And then I would do it again, do it again, do it again. And pretty soon even that loan amount wasn't enough, heaven knows, repaying it and having it replenished every month.

I needed bigger loans to make bigger amounts. Isn't that funny? So, finances are very important and resources, it could be a simple resource like I can go three houses down and get some extra printer paper when I need an extra printer cartridge. It could be a resource like I need a hand truck, I have to move my refrigerator, maybe you've got a sports car and you got a regular sedan or something like that, and you need to get a gas grill for your house. You need somebody that has a pickup truck or you're getting a piece of furniture, your couch won't fit in your trunk. So, resources can be a lot of different things. Resources are almost like the skills areas.

You need somebody that owns a truck when you don't own a truck, you need somebody who has a hand truck when you don't have a hand truck and a ladder when you don't have a ladder. Certain tools when you don't have tools. Somebody has certain computer skills, when you don't have those computer skills, Somebody that does search engine optimization, we don't know how to do that, Somebody that knows how to get certain forms or certain contacts that you need. There's lots of different types of resources. When I was looking for educational jobs, I needed somebody that was in that field that could help me get hooked up and get a job teaching, So, that worked out as well. I made a lot of money teaching, I taught a lot of people, I taught the next generation of therapists, So resources are very, very important. Now, this is just to get you started, here's a few networking options.

One, is "Meetup groups." Simply look up "Meetup Groups." Go ahead and do an internet search in your area for local interests and meet great local people. So, if you want to get connected with people in your area that are doing the same thing that you're doing, this is a great way to make it happen. So, the next one is "LinkedIn." This is an online system for connecting, jobs, questions and answers, research and advice. Let me break this down for you. One of the things that you want to do is just get signed up on LinkedIn, They marked down to FREE (LOL) so, it's right in your price range. Go ahead and do a nice little online profile, put the little picture in and put a few details and some contact information. In like 15 minutes, you're done! Boom! Now, you're on LinkedIn. Now, anytime, anybody is checking you out there in the professional field, whether you're looking for a job or you're looking to get a connection, or somebody just wants to research you, maybe they're checking into you before they do a deal with you. You look professional.

Only the sharpest people, only like the top 10 percent of the people in the country, go to LinkedIn. I don't know what the hell the other 90 percent are doing, but they should be on LinkedIn. Now, I'm going to give you a great tip here. This will be worth the price of the Book by itself. If you love LinkedIn, there is a way to go in through fiverr and as a gig, fiverr is fiverr.com ... They'll do gigs for 5, 10, 15, 20 bucks. Used to be called fiverr because it was all five bucks, no matter how much service you got. Now, they do five bucks and above, so, they've changed their model in the last few months or last couple of years. So, get a gig there that allows you to increase your contacts on LinkedIn automatically. I did this system like eight years ago. I was struggling and struggling. I'd been on Linkedin for like 3-4 years and had probably gotten up to about 150 to 200 contacts in that period of time. Long, slow, ... Slow! It was like walking through mud trying to get my LinkedIn contacts up.

You were considered a "Rock Star" in lInkedin, people start trying to link with you, the whole thing will reverse itself, instead of trying to link in with them, they'll try to link it with you ... When you get 500 or more contacts. It's also going to say, you have 500 plus contacts ... you can have a million. Once you get over that 500, you're in the top 1% or maybe even 1 percent of 1 percent ... but let's say 1 percent, of all the people on LinkedIn. So, now you're sexy as hell, you look great .And you can do this with a fiverr gig in about 3-4 days. So what Fiverr did was they sent me a contact list of people that were in a group called "Lion." I think it was "Linked In Online Network." It was basically people that all agreed in a huge pool that if somebody else that was a "Lion", like yourself, they would always accept their requests, So , they sent me a list of 5000 people that were in the Lion group and all I did is, in bulk, I sent out requests, maybe like a 100 a day, out to these people. I was getting about 80 of them coming back a day. After a couple of days, the other 20 out of each 80 probably came in, and I'll tell you in about 5-6 days, in less than a week, I had 500+ and now I've got several thousand.

People are constantly linking in with me. I don't even fool with it anymore. But I just get a ton of people, and once in a while I go in there and I just add them. Next, anytime you need anything, nationally, internationally, you're connected with everybody. So you can say, "Hey, I've a challenge in this area." You can go to Q&A and just ask a question, put it out there into the universe and you will get a flood, a flood of answers coming back in, from people who are in the top 10 percent of the country. Some people that you couldn't even afford to ask a question to, because they would charge you $300 an hour or more. Also, not only are you going to have contacts for everything you could ever need, want, or desire and I mean multiple contacts, if you use my system right.

When you go for jobs, LinkedIn, very few people know this, and have their own job board. It's really not known out there in the universe, so, you can find jobs on LinkedIn that if you look through all the other major job search engines, you would not find! And here's the bonus, when you find it within LinkedIn, it's going to note everybody that you know in your network that's connected with that company. I'm going to tell you a little tip, there was an old book and they put it out every year since the 80s. I can remember around 1985 I was looking through this book. Even then it was a classic ... It has been out for a couple of years, and every year since they run it, it's called, "What Color Is Your Parachute." And one of the major takeaways from that book is that if you go in for a job interview and you have no reference, your chances of getting that job are somewhere between 1 in 10 to 1 in 20.

So, figure about a one in 15 chance. If you go in, with even a crappy reference, "Hey, I know this guy from the internet, would you take a look at his resume? Would you interview him?" If you get an interview with even a crappy reference, your chances are somewhere between 1 and 2, like 50/50 and 1 in 4, 25 percent. So, say like a 35 percent chance.. That means if you get one, two, three, four interviews, by time you get the fourth interview, normally, you would have had like a 1 in 3 chance of getting a job. Now, you've got a 100 percent chance of getting one job offer, a 50 percent chance of getting two job offers, in like, a 25 percent chance of getting three job offers, hell, you might hit the trifecta and you might get 4 jobs! Who knows? There's a small percentage chance you could hit that as well, so, much better odds on

LinkedIn, So, I hope, I've sold you on LinkedIn and I'll see you in the next chapter.

Specific Time Management Techniques 3

Hey, Everybody welcome back. Keep going and you too will be a "Master of Time Management." Now, in the last chapter, we were talking about LinkedIn and how we could get some questions answered there. But there are some other sites you can use too. I'm going to recommend yahoo answers and ask.com, two great resources. Now, why are they great resources? One, because they save you a boatload of time. Remember my friend Nick said, "If I have to spend more than 5 minutes trying to figure something out with multiple degrees, I'm going to stop and ask somebody who knows." This is a great way to have a network, without having a network, by being able to ask millions of people across the country their answers. Now, people that answer these tend to be higher level, just like LinkedIn. Not quite as much, it depends, but you can get some really good quality answers. What I used to do, and this is the genius system, I mean, literally the "Genius System."

I would be able to look like a "Genius" in almost any situation where I had about 24 hours to answer a question. Why? Say my CEO would ask me a question, or ask maybe all the directors a question, and I would go on LinkedIn, I'll go on yahoo answers, and I would go on Ask.com which I think, used to be "Ask Jeeves" back in the day, if you remember that ... and 24 hours later, I would have this HUGE list of like 50 different answers. I'd narrow it down to the best 3, 5 or 10, whenever I needed for my purposes and then I would present those in front of the board and I would do better than the other 12 directors combined. Why? Because I had a LOT better answers. I had MORE answers. I had HIGHER QUALITY answers.

They didn't even know to look in these areas! So, I would absolutely, positively crush it and come up with some of the best and most creative, most profitable answers you have ever seen. All for FREE! and I looked like a genius. You can too! So, it's an amazingly valuable resource. It would save you money, consulting fees, like I said in the last chapter. Some of these people charge $300 bucks an hour, $500 bucks an hour, to give you these answers and you normally couldn't even get them. It also removes that, "I wish I knew that sooner" feeling. So anytime you get a question on anything, it could be personal health, finance, whatever. Go ahead and check out these sources. You'll never look back and say, "I wish I waited longer."

Go ahead and utilize them. It'll boost your income. It'll save you time. It meets all the criteria. Now, this sheet looks amazingly simple. I did this in outlook and basically, I broke the day into 15 minute increments. And all I would do is, I would put down what I did in that 15 minutes. And then, I had a little insignia that I would make, a little note to myself, maybe a check mark or an X, "Would you pay somebody to do this?" So, if it's waiting in line at the grocery store. No, that's not making me money. I'm losing money. If it's sitting there waiting for copies to come out of the copier, I'm losing money, I'm not making money. You say, "Well, you got to make the copies." No, you turn on the copy machine. You don't have to WAIT for the copies. See, how does this work? They did a study in Time Management with the average worker.

And all they did is, they had a stopwatch and they started it every time somebody did something that you PAY him for and they stopped it, every time somebody wasn't doing something you paid him for. They found that people were working less than 25% of the time! That wasn't a bad worker ... That was an AVERAGE worker. You've got to use this time management sheet. If you use this for anything, like a week or two weeks, you will have plus or minus 5 percent, everything nailed down for what are at least 80 or 90 percent of your time wasters. I call this the system by which you find "The holes in your boat." Where is your time leaking out and falling on the ground? This is how you do it. Just do these sheets even for three or four days.

Why not be 80 percent accurate? Do it for a week or two, you'll be about 90 to 95 percent accurate, because most things that are ever going to happen, happen in a week or two, so, you'll get very good results. You will be amazed before you get through the end of your first day, you'll already start to see where you're losing time and you'll be like, "Oh my god, I did not know it was this bad!" Then do it to get better and it kind of pushes yourself so you won't lose as much time. The average person, because you're even thinking about it, this sheet will actually be a little bit off. Even the first time you use it, you know why? Because when you use a time tracker sheet, What are you thinking about? You're thinking about tracking your time ... and you'll want to look good, Yeah. Even just focusing on Time Management by doing this sheet here, will usually increase your productivity about 25 percent, Boom! On day one.

So actually, no matter how much time you thought you lost, when you did the sheet, when you tallied up at the end of the day, you would have lost 25% more on an average day. And you know it's true, yeah, absolutely. So, time tracker, absolutely crucial. Make sure you use it and you will do amazing. I'll try to leave you a copy of this in the resource chapter or in the bonus chapter, depending on which platform you buy this off of. But I'll try to have this hidden away somewhere that you can find it and download it, and utilize it, beautiful sheet. Now, this is my patented "Walk and Talk System", I invented this. People would say,

"Hey , can I talk to you about a blank" and I say, "Sure, walk and talk" which meant I wasn't even going to slow down to talk to them.

So it's a huge time saver, keeps conversations short, keeps them targeted and gives people more respect for your time. How does that work? When I say, "ok, fine. Walk and Talk." What do they know? They've got between now and when I hit my destination ... I could hit my destination in 5 seconds or it could be 20 seconds ... but it isn't going to be very long, no more than 30 seconds. I mean, how long is this building, right? Thirty seconds. You can walk about half a block in 30 seconds. So people know that they've got to be tight, so keep the conversation short, they stay on target. They're not going to B.S., they're not going to ask you about the weather.

They're going to come right to the what? To the "Ask," what do you need? Huge, huge time saver. Make sure you use this one and use it on a daily basis. Next one is "Eliminate Problems That Repeat." I love this one. This is a huge time saver. You got to use this one. So ask yourself 2 questions. What problems have you been staring at? ... Which means just watching them repeat over and over again and what problems are your staff staring at. They're watching them repeat over and over again and what? NOT telling you! "It's a secret ... don't tell the boss." Or they don't think to tell you, they think this is just natural or normal. NO, losing time, like losing money, is never normal! If you are leaking blood out of somewhere, would you consider that normal? NO, money is what? The "lifeblood" of any business.

If you're leaking money, it's like somebody stabbed you and they're sucking the life out of you, :(So, when problems repeat, you've got to nail them down. Something happens once in a while, it's a rarity, don't get too nervous about it. Handle it the best you can and forget about it. But the things that repeat are costing you time. Say something costs you five minutes a day, ok, well, that's 25 minutes a week because it happens once a day. 25 minutes a week times 52 weeks in a year is 1,300 minutes divide that by 60, over 21.5 hours! So, why wouldn't you solve something like that when you can get 21 and a half hours back in the next year? And it might take you 3 hours to figure out how to solve it.

Something like that, something is small, something that takes up as little as five minutes. 21 and a half hours. 21.6 hours a year. Take one, two or three or four or five hours whatever you have to do to nail it down. Now, what if this is five minutes times everyone of your staff and there's 20 of them? Well now, you lost about 410 hours, 420 hours. Somewhere in there, that's a lot of—pay! So, don't stare at problems that repeat. Go through and assess current problems with your team. Find out what they are. Create an action plan on how we're going to deal with it step by step.

Accountability. Who is going to do what and when. Monitor it. "What's not monitored, doesn't get done," Right? That's gotten to your area, right? And then follow up, make sure they're doing ok. Make sure they don't need any help. Make sure they're getting it done and give them some encouragement. Tell me did a great job of this, show some of these figures, how much they're saving. They're doing wonderful work and they're saving you a ton of money, So, whether in your life or as part of a team make sure you use this system. It will save you a boatload of time. You'll never look back and say, "I wish I didn't do this." This is one of the ways that you "fill the holes in your boat" that you find through your time tracker sheet.

Specific Time Management Techniques 4

Hey everybody, welcome back! You're doing absolutely amazing, you're more than halfway through ... So I'm very proud of you. Now, this is going to seem like a funny little technique, but it is huge, "Find A Good Hiding Place." I love this graphic here. Looks like George Clooney there, doesn't it? Here's the deal. You can get more done in a focused hour alone, than you can in 2 to 3 hours dealing with interruptions and distractions. I had a buddy. His name was Nick. And what he did was, he actually took the expense to rent an office, one floor down from where he actually worked. What he would do is, he would sneak down there for an hour once, twice, three times a day and he could get everything done. He could get two - three hours worth of work done in that amount of time, in that one hour.

So 1 hour became 2-3 easily, sometimes 4-5. He had a lot of distractions. He tried to train people not to distract him, but against all resistance. they would always push through in some way, shape or form, So find a good hiding place. I did that when I was working at a mental health facility. There was a doctor's office, and the doctor was only in there for about 3 hours a week to check out the patients. And I think they used a little bit on the weekends for something. But 95.5% of the time ... That place was empty. If I ever wanted to go down and lie on the cot and relax my back, take a breather, or relieve stress, I could do that there. If I just wanted an empty space to get a lot of work done, I could do that there.

There was a conference room that they would use three or four hours of the day, you got to realize 16 hours in two shifts, so about 80 percent of the time that was free if you just knew when the meetings were. So I could ask the administrative assistant who knows anybody to use this for the next hour or so? Sometimes I would even tape over the windows or I would sit down at the far end so that when they looked through that little glass pane they couldn't see me at the far end. They would think the room was empty when it wasn't.

Sometimes people would sneak in to use it for something or have a conversation or I don't know what they were going to do. And there's an old person sitting there and my boss thought it was impressive that I was getting away, getting things focused, getting things done, taking special time to figure out ways to work harder and more effectively. That was worth a promotion right there. So great, great technique. Don't fail to use this. It will serve you very, very well. I love this graphic don't you. I mean sometimes it feels like this is what it's getting down to, right? You've got a plan stress breaks into your day. What happens is over the day your stress goes up and up and up.

And if you don't do some kind of pattern interrupt, you don't take a little stress break, you don't knock that down .... It's going to get high, Stay high and burn you out! Remember the stress mantra is "Anything worth doing, is worth overdoing." I was one of these people. I'm as guilty as anybody. If there was a stress gang, I was the leader of it. I loved to eat stress. I would tell people out, they would say, How's everything going?" I'd say, "Great! I'm burning the candle on both ends and down the middle and hitting the rest with a flamethrower" I love stress. Love to overdo it. Love to be hard charging, made me feel good. I Liked to have too much caffeine.

I liked to be kicking things out, making other people look really slow. Getting an amazing amount done & feeling fantastic. When I leave, I know I absolutely, positively crushed. Well, I'll tell you, do that for about the first 10 years of your career, you're fine, you won't even notice it. Around year 15-20 you're going to get major burnout, anxiety disorder, depression and you're going to start slowing down. It's going to start interrupting your thinking, your creativity is going to go to pot,

Take the stress breaks! What studies have found is, if you take like four short stress breaks, maybe three minutes, might be five minutes. We're only talking about anywhere from 10 to 15 minutes a day. That is one tenth of a percent of your day.

It's very, very small, just a teeny tiny fraction. And what happens is your productivity. You know, say that's 3 percent of your day, but your productivity will go up 10, 15, 20, sometimes 25 percent. You'll come up with better ideas, you'll be more creative, you'll last longer. If you do have to do some extra hours that day, You won't be as tired. You'll sleep better at night. You'll be better to your family when you go home. They say they have "the strongest metal wear with use," it's the strongest battery will drain with use. You have to recharge your batteries a little bit. People tell you this. They tell you this like it's a relaxation thing or it's going to keep your anxiety down.

And people who are hard charging arelike, "NO! That's the minute I take advantage of everybody when they're resting, I'm kicking—!" Now, the people that are the most effective because, remember, Time Management is about working SMARTER not necessarily harder. The people that are hard working and don't look left or right, they're just kicking it out, trying to get that last little advantage. They don't slow down long enough to make sure that they're using good systems, to make sure they're heading in the right direction, to check and see how well they're doing, to look around and see what other resources they could be using. Usually during these times of quiet rest, I can almost guarantee, at least half the time, you're going to come up with an idea that will save your time, today, tomorrow, the next day while you're relaxing. Because an idea would just float to your mind, when you finally calm your mind down, because your mind when you're getting this stress, it tightens, and tightens and pretty soon, new and creative ideas can't get through that net.

But by relaxing, a great idea that will save you several multiples of the time you took off to relax, will float into your mind. Sometimes life changes, So don't think stress breaks are for sissies who can't take stress. They are for people who want to be the most efficient. It's like Stephen Covey used to say in the book, Seven Habits Of Highly Effective People, he said, "If I had an hour to chop down a tree and spend the first 50 minutes sharpening the ax." The stress breaks are for you to sharpen the ax. Take care of the tool that does all that hard work, so it can keep doing it. Come up with those creative ideas that float in, in between and do your absolute best work. You'll also find, you'll make less mistakes. If it takes you five minutes to do something, you make a mistake, and It will take you 25 to 30 minutes, five to six times as long just to fix that. Why? You were going too fast! You didn't take any breaks, You didn't relax and watch what you're doing ... and it will hurt you.

Now, here's your next major time thief, TV. The average person spends 3 hours per day in front of the TV. This is huge! Check yourself. How much time did you spend? Is it two hours? Three hours? four hours? Remember, this is the average person, we only worry about you! So, if you could take back just a half hour per day, from watching the TV. This is going to give you an extra three and a half hours per week. That is 182 hours per year! That's an entire month of 40 hours a week work. Do the math! See if I got it right. That's a boatload of time. I can teach you a quick trick right here. Be worth the price Of course, just to learn this. Here's what you do. Watch your three hours of TV but here's what I want you to do ... RECORD it. Don't watch anything live! Here's how TV works. 60 Minutes is one hour, one show, ok, or two half hour shows.

Let's say, it's a 60 minute show. How much time is 60 Minutes commercials? 20 minutes! You get to watch two minutes for every one that they take. They give you 2, you pay for one. That's 20 minutes out of every hour! So in three hours, you can get an hour back ... or two months worth of work ... Per year. Just by watching pre-recorded and skipping past the commercials. Beautiful way to do it! So I'm not saying watch less TV ... but do it more efficiently. And then Of course, if you want to, go ahead and watch a lot of TV. It won't hurt you. Nobody's ever died from watching too little TV. You'll never see that in the papers. TV is a major time thief. And spend some time on TV watching something that's going to HELP you with your life, so it can be equally entertaining. What I do is, I love the Netflix documentaries. They have lots of great stuff on health, and wealth, and finance, and relationships, and psychology, things that will help you make money or improve your life in some way, shape or form.

I've been pouring through recently, just hours and hours and hours, of diet & nutrition. Because I have a sound mind, I want to die of natural causes. I want to save a bunch of time. I want to make a bunch of money. I want to enjoy my life. I want to die from old age. Many of these things that make you decrepit ... don't have to ... They are entirely preventable, through a tiny amount of exercise, diets and a few very simple supplements. That's what I want to have going on in my life, So I take a chunk of my normal TV time and I pour it into it. I'll even take some of my TV time, because the last thing that we were talking about was stress management, and at the end of the night, for about 10 maybe 15 minutes ... I'll watch a relaxation tape, like the ocean or a fireplace, those are my two favorite.

There's a babbling brook one that I like sometimes and I watch that to decompress from the TV, to de-stress myself, before I go to bed, So, just a little bonus tip for you there. Let's move on to your next tip ... got another great one here for you. This is a major in the field of Time Management. It's called "Batch Tasking." So what you do, is you take all your tasks and you put them into batches. Take all your phone messages and return all your phone messages at once. Do all your filing at once.

Do all your copying at once. Do all your progress notes or filling out forms all at once. Do all your paperwork all at once. What happens is, you can see on this learning curve, This is an actual learning curve. Each time you do something, the first and second time. These are practices, they're considered, if I do three or four more of those, you can see the amount of time it takes is dropping.

If I do it five or six times , or practice as they call them, drops, drops, drops. So, by the time you get out to about 10 or 12, you just about maxed it out, certainly by 13 or 15, you pretty much maxed out any benefits. But if you start and stop ... you do a few messages, then you do a little bit of paperwork, then you do a little bit of your copies, then you do a little bit of your filing. This gives you a little bit more variety, and people tend to like this better, but I'm not going to like it better if it's taking me, and look at that learning curve. you got it down to about a minute a task, down from seven minutes. So, it's going to take me somewhere between half the time and a third of the time, if you kind of do the math on this to do it in batches.

And if that's not exciting enough for you, you're going to have a half to two thirds of that time. It took you an hour, you'll be done in about 20 minutes and somebody else it'll still take them another 40 minutes, you go do something fun for that 40 minutes and still be done as soon as they are. Or you can say hey, I'm going to take that 40 minutes, I'm going to blow 20 minutes of it and just enjoy myself and kind of laugh at the fools that don't do it this way. I'm going to take the 20 minutes left, and I'm going to get ahead of them, and beat them every single time. Even though I took 20 minutes off! They are too—slow. Why? They weren't smart enough to take a time management class! They weren't smart enough to listen to the instructor and start batching the tasks. They don't know about efficiency, they don't know about the learning curve. This is why this program is giving you an unfair advantage in life! So, remember batching tasks and you will absolutely crush them.

Specific Time Management Techniques 5

Hey, folks we are rolling right along and the great tips just keep on coming. Now, your briefcase, remember it's a tool, it's not storage. Remember a briefcase can save you time or it can waste it. Tips. Keep it organized, you want to be able to find things fast, simple and easy. Keep it well stocked. Make sure that you have everything that you need in there to be efficient. Make sure you also don't have things in there that you don't need. So always ask yourself, what do I need for the task? Make sure that's the only thing in there. I used to keep a box by my desk and all the extra stuff in my briefcase, when I was going to an important meeting, I would dump it out so I had just the things that I needed for the task.

Later I would fill it back in, because I loved it to kind of be like a Swiss army knife. I want to have a stapler when I need it. I had a little mini one that I wanted to have for the ruler. I want to have some of the extras and niceties that I had in my briefcase and extra notebooks and some guides that I had, I always had those. Things that made me efficient, things that were going to make me money, not just any old thing, not old paper work. Keep it neat, keep it clean, keep it organized. You'll be glad you did. Huge time saver. Now, here's one of the most shocking things you're ever going to see. The stopwatch technique, I alluded to briefly in a previous chapter. I said, they did a study and all they did is they followed staff around with a stopwatch and every time they did something that they would pay them for they started the stopwatch, tick, tick, tick, tick, tick and every time they were wasting time, were doing something that I would not pay you for.

Boom, off it went, clock runs when you're doing something that I would pay you for, It stops when you're doing something, I wouldn't. They found that the average person was only working 25 percent of that time. That's two hours out of an eight hour shift, you're packing two hours into eight hours and you go home at night and you tell your wife, boy I had a horrible day today, they just ran me ragged. No, you have horrible time management. You don't even understand how much time you're wasting. You've got to do this sometime and this will show you how bad your time management is. It'll get you focused on making it better, in between this and the time tracker, the time management sheet that I gave you, these two techniques, you will be crushing it in the area of time management.

You'll have a greater awareness of where all the holes in your boat are, where all the time is leaking out and an intolerance of the things that are wasting your time. These little conversations about minutia and the weather and it'll drive you nuts when you see people at the copier, just watching the copier, copy, they're watching another device do work while they're doing nothing and guess what? That stopwatch goes off. I used to figure out other things that I could do with the copier. I didn't care if I was just educating myself and reading something while I was at the copier. Sometimes I'd bring a little filing box and I do some filing or I get on my cell phone and I start returning some of the calls, and some of the messages, or I'd start doing some notes, or planning, or strategizing, or doing some paperwork at the copier.

I would use my briefcase as a little desk, I'd open it up and then I'd close it and I'd use it for a little desk and I'd write on top of it and I would start getting things done. People are like, why are you not doing that in your office? Well, because I'm making copies, if I were in my office, I'd be working there but until they move the copier into my office, it's not going to happen or I would go to the copier. I would get the copies running, go back to my office, get some work done and then go back to the copier. Long as it wasn't too far away. Now, this would drive people nuts because if he got there in 20 to 30 seconds had gone by and was waiting for the copier and they're like, "What's all this stuff in there?"

They're so mad but oh, well because they're all going to be working for me someday. Why? Because I have excellent time management, so use a stopwatch technique.

Use it to find your wasted time and get that time. Remember time is life. Get that back. Now, there's two types of conversations in life. If you do a sitting conversation, the same conversation, getting the same amount done on average statistically, 10 to 20 minutes, so figure 15 minutes. Standing conversation, having this exact same conversation, Standing up, in the same place you're at or in the hall or in your office, doesn't matter ... 3 to 4 minutes to get it done. When people sit down, they get social, they relax, they talk about a lot of extra things. Have your conversation standing. When I used to have people that came into my office and wasted my time, the first thing I did is, I shot out of my chair, went over to the door to greet him, said "Hi" and said "How can I help you today?" Which meant getting right into the conversation. "Hi" is all the niceties we're going to have.

I didn't even say "Hello", because "Hi" was shorter. (LOL) So, I wanted to be standing. And if they were taking too long, I want to be standing and I wanted to be up so I could walk out the door. I would tell them that I had to go, do something, be some place, maybe go to copier, make another copy. But I wanted to get them OUT of my office. So, that's kind of 2 techniques and one. Remember, sitting is going to be about 5 times longer! Figure 4 to 5 times longer. Standing, 4 to 5 times what? Shorter! You're going to get this done at about 20 to 25 percent of the time! So, have standing conversations. I used to do this as a technique when companies were hire me to go in as a consultant. They would say, we have these board meetings and they go on and on and on. They're set for like an hour, an hour and a half, and they end up going like, two, three hours. They're just getting to be too—long, we don't get through half our agenda.

First thing I would do is have everybody come into the room and we would do two things. We would set an AGENDA, great time saver, right? And then we would do the entire meeting STANDING, perfect. Standing is always better. When people were standing, I guarantee you that in that hour-long conference, people can't stand for more than about half an hour at a whack, and they're very uncomfortable. That hour meeting got condensed down a half an hour and 100 percent everything got done, because we told them everything on the agenda had to get done. Do you know how much time saving that was? We got done more in 25 percent of the time that they were spending, than they were getting in a 100% of the time, So in an hour, an hour and a half, they didn't get as much done as we got done in about 20 or 30 minutes, that's about when their legs gave out.

Now, here's another huge time saver. Because remember, time and money are the SAME thing. I hope you're not just working to work, unless you're a humanitarian, or you're doing really good work like I did therapy. So I would do some extra hours, get paid, didn't get paid, didn't matter. I loved to do the work. I want to do high quality work, so I was willing to do that. But otherwise, I get paid hourly, and I don't work more than you pay me. And I always want to get paid more and more. So, I have to be worth more and more. So, if time is money, you should be building your financial skills. You're working for your money ... but your money should be working for you. This is a time condenser. It's going to condense the time until you're wealthy, until your income and investments are actually making more than your job and it's going to condense the time between now and when you get to retire.

Did I mention it's going to condense the time between now and when you get to retire? I hope you heard that! So, a strange piece, but financial skills are actually time management. So, get into a couple of things. Mutual funds. Mutual funds are awesome, because before the 80s, when I was kind of getting out there in the workaday world, I think around 1980 to 85, somewhere in there, is when all the mutual funds were coming out. You used to have to buy stocks in blocks of 10,000. Or if you had a body or a broker that would be kind enough to break it down from a 10,000 block to 5,000. To get one block of shares, say it was. It was a 10000 block of shares. If it was like a crappy penny stock, that was like, $3, you had to come up with $30,000! And did you have a diversity if that stock went to hell? What happened to your money? It went to hell too! Now, you can spend the opposite.

You can spend like $30 or $50 and put it in a mutual fund and you could spread it like, I want one one millionth of a share and spread it over like 10 or 15 different stocks. You can have amazing diversity. You don't invest either just when you have a block of 30,000, or 50,000 ,or 100,000 to invest. Every time. You know, you could be putting in an extra 20, 40, 50 bucks a week and invest, invest, invest, beautiful way. Mutual funds are the greatest thing ever invented. Here's another great invention, Iras, Individual Retirement Accounts. Basically, they're on their way to instantly make your tax bracket back on your money in ONE second! Say you're in a 30% tax bracket, you're making, what would that be, around $50 - $60,000 a year. That probably puts you in a 30% tax bracket. Now, it's graduated, they don't charge that and say maybe like the first $25,000. So your effective rate isn't 30%, It's more like 20 percent.

So for every hundred dollars, I put away into an IRA, the government would have taken in $20 bucks anyways. So, no. When I keep it as income, I have a hundred dollars but they only give me 80 and the government takes 20. When I put it into an IRA, the WHOLE hundred goes in there and I get to keep it! So what does that mean? It means INSTANTLY, in a second, by putting it in there, I made 20% on my money! That's amazing! Try to show me an investment, guaranteed, rock solid, cannot fail ... Guaranteed 20 percent. Hard to find! If you could find that, you could sell it in the open market for billions of dollars. You'd be the richest man in the country. Hard to find and it never lasts. Ira's been doing this for decades now.

And every year, normally, say, you made $100 on your investments. The government would come in and take, I think the current rates around 24%, they would take 24 dollars out of every hundred that you earned by being smart and having your investments. So if you make 100 bucks, no, the government only says, you can only keep $76 of that. In a normal investment, that's true. In an IRA they let you keep 100%! So say, I'm making 8 percent of my IRA and you're making 10 percent on yours individually. You're actually going to end up with a few less dollars than I am. Because you're losing 24 percent and there's only a spread of 20 percent between us. I'm actually, even though I'm making 20% percent less, I'm actually making 4% more than you! So, IRAs make 20 percent right off the bat minimum, more if you're in a higher tax bracket. And it's going to accumulate wealth, without taxes.

You don't get taxed on this, until you retire, and then at a lower rate. So, you save a huge amount. Now, taxes are a huge amount of income. You got to get real good at hiding your money and avoiding some of these taxes. One of the best ways, bar none is the IRAs. Say, if I hit $60000 this year, I'll end up jumping up a tax bracket, and paying another 5 percent. So, last year I made $55,000 ... No problem. This year, I got a promotion and I got a raise or whatever. Now I'm at 60,000, ooh. I'm going to give up most of that 5000, maybe like $4,000 out of the $5,000 ...because I jumped tax brackets. Here's what I can do. Put like a thousand dollars in an IRA. That is not considered part of your taxable income. Now, it looks like you only made $59,000 this year.

So, you're going to save that 20% on the thousand, you're going to make income on that over time like we talked about, and you dropped yourself in a tax bracket! So, get good with taxes. That's just ONE tax tip. Get together with your accountant and get on line, get educated, take a Book on it, get really good at it. The next area for most people that have massive wealth, real estate is a big part. So, Of course getting your own home can be part of that. You could buy into real estate. There's lots of different ways to do real estate. You'd be surprised, real estate isn't just buying a place and renting it. No. There's about a million different ways to do real estate.

So check into that, look into that, build up your financial skills. These are just a few examples. But you've got to get really good at doing one or two things, making more money by having your money make you money, or getting out there working more what? More time, more hours! That's why this is part of Time Management. It is a huge part of it because like I said, it can seriously cut down the amount of time it takes between now and when you retire.

Specific Time Management Techniques 6

Hey, everybody. Welcome back. You're just in time for snacks. I call this chapter Lunch versus crunch. I used to love to keep some snacks around. I would do dry goods in my car, especially because I live in Florida. Sometimes the heat is just intense. Chocolate's not going to make it. Chips aren't going to make it. But some dry goods, especially granola bars and those types of things, beautiful seeds and nuts would do very well in this environment. All depends on the temperature. But most places don't put chocolate in your car. But in the car in the office, this can be a huge time saver when you just don't have time for lunch or, you know, I a lot of times wouldn't have much for breakfast. I have a granola bar, maybe a granola bar or a sandwich or a light salad for lunch.

And then I have my main meal at dinner. So a lot of times if I was going to skip something, I want to have some snacks around. I didn't want to pay extra for them, so I would buy them in bulk. I tried to make sure they were healthy so I wasn't eating junk. I always made sure I had some bottled water around and it just saved me time, money and hassle. I never had to go out to the store. I never paid extra because if you pay extra, you gotta do what? Work more hours, spend more time paying for this junk, and never, ever, ever go out to lunch unless you're making money doing it. I would sit down with a gorgeous lunch. I could cook it and eat it in about five, 10 minutes.

My wife made it for me and the cost of making that meal was probably about $1.30 5 to 2 bucks. Somebody goes to McDonald's, they eat a pile of crap. It's five bucks. It's almost six bucks after tax. They've got to take 15 minutes to go to McDonald's, 15 minutes to come back, 5 minutes wait in line, 15 minutes eating their meal. And this is like a 45 minute to an hour adventure. And they call that fast food. How can that be? Me at my desk having a healthy lunch or a tasty snack. That was the way to do it. Save me a boatload of time, a boatload of money. I once calculated that people were spending approximately 1000 to $2000 per year. It was closer to about 1500, maybe 1700, if they put that away every single year. That's the difference in the price of their lunch versus my lunch. That was probably about half of what they needed to retire on.

Yeah, it was about $1000 to $500 somewhere in there. You do the math. You see what you come up with. Again, what does that do? That's more time when I've already got enough money to retire. They're 40, 50, trying to put away five, six times as much, doing massive hours, doing overtime, all this type of junk when they should be slowing down in their career. Okay. They're spending more time trying to make up for the retirement money that they lost and they lost it with stupid stuff: magazines, cell phones, snacks, lunches, and a lot of it was just going out to lunch. These people weren't even making that much money. They're going out to lunch every day.

I'm like, That's a rich man's sport. I take my wife out to dinner about once a month or, you know, we do one thing a week, that's it, you know, because it's just too expensive. And even when it isn't, I just get bored doing this stuff. I don't like to eat out every night of the week. That's crazy. I hate it when I have to do that when I'm in hotels, so. Major convenience. Major cost saver. Major time saver. Lunch versus crunch. Now, when you've got people working for you always give clear instructions. Okay, maybe not that clear. Don't do the bullhorn here. But there was a weird study and it showed that you had to say something to somebody four times for them to get 100% once. So what I would typically do is I would give people very clear instructions.

I would break it down. You need to do step one, step two, step three, step four. And then I would ask them, are there any questions? And they would say, no. And I would say, okay, tell me back what I just told you. And about two thirds of the time they would get it wrong. And I'd say, okay. And I go back over it. A lot of times I don't even bother if I'm giving this assignment to three or four people or sometimes even one, because I don't want to lose the hours. Either they're man hours or my man hours. They have to fix it or to tell them again or to reassign it, I'll write the—thing down for them. Because like I said, I could tell him like three times before or four times before they get it even once. So don't say, Oh, I told so-and-so to do that. He should have it done.

Oh, no, no, no, no. That's going to blow back on you. And I want you to take full responsibility for that. Not because you didn't tell them you did, but did you tell them three or four times? Did you write it down? Did you train them on it? Did you check and monitor to make sure they did it? If you didn't do all those things, it's not their fault. It's your fault. That's why you're management. Now, having said that, if you're a line worker, if you're working under somebody, which is what? Because jobs are pyramid schemes, virtually everybody is under somebody. When the boss gives you instructions, he's going to think he can just tell you once, slow the roll, ask them questions, take it down, and he'll say, I just want you to do a great job on this. Slow him down.

What would a great job look like? Okay. How much time have you budgeted for this? Um. How often do you want me to check these types of things? What are the exact outcomes you want from each one of these steps? Slow them down. Make sure they are clear. Bosses are not always good at giving instructions. Now screening phone calls is another huge, huge timesaver. Taking a call will actually extend the length of the call three times. That's what studies show. That's an actual number. Taking the call will make it three times longer, so only pick up on the most vital calls. So if the boss calls or supplier calls or a major buyer calls, take those calls. But everybody else, let them go to the answering machine. Then we're going to do what? We're going to batch our tasks. We're going to answer our calls.

Now, this helps you and it helps them. Why? Because you'll be able to listen to their message, figure out exactly what they need. Get them those things without any small talk. And have everything lined up and done for them and then call them and tell them it's already over. You've solved it. They'll be thrilled. As far as they're concerned, they weren't even thinking about it. You called them and you instantly solved it. You did it fast. You saved their time. You saved your time. And you were most efficient with the company time and the company resources.

So remember, phone calls are a major time thief. Only pick up on the most vital ones. Now this seems like a strange time management piece, but use surge protectors. This is kind of an odd one. See last known location of your computer when that blows up, when it takes everything, you better have used a surge protector. Matter of fact, I would go the extra step, spend about 150 bucks. People were amazed when I did this. I spent 150 bucks when the power went out in the building. I had a backup laptop for my desktop so I could go about an hour and a half on that. And even my desktop, I could keep running for about an hour and a half off the battery in low power mode pool. So I was able to go up to 3 hours of working when basically everybody else got sent home for the day.

They're like, What can we do? Everybody was milling around in their office saying, Well, you know, by candlelight, I can do a little bit of paperwork or, you know, phones came back after an hour. I could do a little bit of that or I could make some calls on my cell phone or whatever. But basically, they were all screwed. I didn't miss a beat. And I'm in Florida. Power will go out three, four, five, six times a year. Or because you don't have the battery backup or you don't have the surge protector, it will crash your system and you won't have the backup.

You're going to lose whatever you're working on. So I'll give you one little more bonus time management tip under this one. Go into like, say, if you're using Microsoft Word and Microsoft Office, you can go under settings and options. And set it to make sure that it makes a backup copy of all your work. It saves your work. You could do it like once a minute. I think that's a strain on the system.

I said it for about 3 to 5 minutes. Three is better. It takes about a split second for the computer to do that. You won't even notice the drain and resources. And boom, boom, boom. You won't lose more than 3 to 5 minutes worth of work. Perfect. That's your tip for this chapter, and I'll see you in the next part of the chapter.

Specific Time Management Techniques 7

Hey, welcome back. More specific Time Management Techniques. This one is batching trips and planning the routes. Trips are major time wasters, so you always want to keep your travel to a bare minimum, So, what I do is I always try to plan the route and batch all my trips together. Get from point A to Point B in the shortest distance and least amount of time possible. Why do I do this? Because I want to save time, money, and gas. I mean, if you look at gas prices lately, they're through the roof, they're terrible. So, beat the system. Many times because you're wasting your staff's time. It's better to host the meeting. So, a lot of people thought I was generous. "'s so nice he always hosts the meeting and he puts out nice snacks and blah, blah, blah, blah, blah." If you look at the time spent, it took my staff half an hour to go to somebody else's place, get settled in and start the meeting, and then a half an hour back. That's one man hour.

Say you're paying your staff $20 an hour a piece and you've got to send 5 staff members over there and it wastes an hour, 20 times 5, that's $100 bucks, I can buy a lot of snacks for 30 bucks. Get five more hours of productive time from my staff, and only spend 30 bucks. And I don't have to pay the mileage, or trip time or any of that stuff. Boom, done! That's why, I'll tell you, It very quickly becomes much more efficient and much cheaper to be able to host the meeting. So, your tips on travel. Next tip is to hire an assistant or two. You've got two right here. There you go. Think of it this way, if you're making $40 per hour or more, Why are you doing $20 per hour tasks? Redo the math. What you want to do is take who you are and multiply it. Now, I learned a great way to do this through "Virtual Assistants." I have Virtual Assistants over in the Philippines.

So I pay them anywhere from $1.50 which is a normal wage. Actually, I think I pay them $1.75, because $1.50 is a normal wage over there. So, I want to start him out at a good wage that they're happy with, and they'll be loyal. Then if they do good work, Of course, I bump them up from there. So, that's very cheap. I don't know if you can afford $20 per hour for a normal American assistant, but you certainly can with virtual assistance. So, start with virtual assistance, and then for the things you absolutely positively must have somebody here, hire somebody. Pay under the table, whatever you need to do. Did the IRS hear that? No. Ok. Do what you need to do. Don't spend your time doing work that is at a lower pay rate than you. Making copies is like minimum wage work. You know it's $10, maybe $15 an hour. You can't make $40 an hour or $100 an hour, if you're doing $15 in $10 an hour work! So always do that math, always check that out. So how can you multiply yourself by getting cheaper staff? Lawyers are the best at this! You know what they'll do? They will charge you $300 bucks an hour.

They'll charge you for a minimum of 10 hours, they're going to spend maybe 45 minutes with you. They're going to hire somebody at $35 bucks an hour. That's called a legal assistant, right? Legal aid. And they're going to do the other 9.25 hours with you. See how much money they're making? You think they're making $300 bucks an hour? Oh, no, no, no. They're making several multiples of that! You can see how they barely worked one hour to make ten. That's like them making what? $3,000 dollars an hour! And what's their expense out of that? Thirty five times nine ... maybe out of that $3000 I have to pull out a couple of hundred. But I'm still making $2,800 dollars an hour versus $300. So, if you ever thought they were expensive before, look at what they actually do and you'll be amazed! They're basically signing off on legal assistance.

That's what you should be doing! How can I be making money where people are paying me, say, 100 bucks an hour to do something ... and pay somebody else $20 bucks an hour to get it done. I quickly check over maybe five, six, seven, eight, nine, ten people's work. I get 80 percent of five, six, seven, eight, nine, ten people's work. I now have like 8 times as much money and I haven't done one more bit of work. This is one of your major, major time management skills. Get people working for you, inexpensively, but pay them well. They're inexpensive compared to you. You keep becoming more valuable, make your services more valuable, so you can charge more and more, and more, and people will beat a path to your door. Then, lower paid people do all the work and you just check it, perfectly.

Now, this has always been a major bone of contention with people. People say, "Oh, a clean desk is a sign of a sick mind." (LOL) That sounds funny when you say it ... but it's not actually true. Messy desks are major time wasters. They even checked this with people that have messy desks. They let them have their messy desk and they check their productivity, and then they clean their desks, get organized, and check it afterwards. On average, even for somebody that's really good at handling a messy desk ... 20 to 25 percent boost in efficiency. Nice! And nothing ever gets lost. Second thing, if you're not good with handling a messy desk, but things just get away from you. You're going to see an even greater increase in productivity.

Which is what? Time savings, money! So try to keep a neat office. Buy a couple of simple organizers. I don't care if you put things in boxes, but get them squared away. We seem like we never want to slow down long enough to spend an hour or two organizing our desks to save a couple hundred hours by the end of the year. But do it, do it, do it. Make it happen. Now, a little bit about the cleanup. Remember we just talked about a messy office? Yes! I've got something for you called the "TRAF System." T - R - A - F. Let me walk you through it. You're going through all this junk on your desk, in your office, and your filing cabinets. So, the first thing is the "circular file" also known as "T" for Trash. What would happen? What's the worst thing that would happen if I lost this item? Ok.

And what are the chances that that will happen? Do that math in your head, and if at all possible, when in doubt ... throw it in the trash! If you're not going to throw it in the trash. And you say there's a 1 in 100 chance that I might need this, or this could be a major liability if I ever lost this, not one chance in a hundred or one chance in a thousand that it ever needed, but let's hold on to it. Put that in a "trash box." Almost like you would do a 'recycle bin,' but don't keep it in with your regular desk stuff. Don't keep it in your files. It's something you can pour through if there was an emergency, but keep it in a box. I guarantee at the end of the year, you'll be able to throw all that stuff safely out, but it won't be cluttering up all your day to day stuff. Next, try to refer to as many things as you can.

Your job is not to do your job... It's to send it to somebody else that's less important than you! (LOL) Always delegate, delegate, delegate! So, I've got a bunch of things that need to be done. I got a bunch of paperwork, I'm going to trash as much as I can. I'm going to refer some stuff out. Next, if you have some paperwork on your desk or in your files, take some action on it - so you can get rid of it and anything that you can't take action on. Well, think of it this way, if I can't trash it, I can't give it to somebody else to take care of, I can't take care of it myself. Guess what? File it! Don't leave it out, file it. Do this system, you'll have massive productivity gains, you'll have less challenges, less things will get lost, you're just going to feel better, breathe better. Hell, you might look better! (LOL) Enjoy this tip. This will save you a ton of time, a ton of hassles.

Specific Time Management Techniques 8

Everybody, here's your next great tip. Create templates. Think about how many different templates you can create for things that you do over and over, and over again. Remember, I said problems that repeat need to be addressed? Well, tasks that repeat, like templates, things that use forms, Power Points, could be emails. All these things can be what they call "Templatized." Simply made into templates, where you have a template, and just alter it slightly and it saves you a boatload of time and always comes out perfect, always comes out gorgeous. Try to think of how many different things you can create templates of and make it happen. Great little tip, great little time saver. Here's another great time saver, learn how to say "no" or Hell no! Minimally, say no. People are such people pleasers.

They have a hard time saying no. People say, "Can you help me with this?" and I say, "no." I can pass you over to somebody that'll help you. I can give you a tip on how to help you. Or maybe this is just something you need to do on your own. Be comfortable saying no. With or without helping them, with or without an excuse. Sometimes the simple answer is "No." Somebody says, "Will you give a dollar to this charity." Answer is no, "could you give me a hand with this?" No. That's it. You don't need to say anything else. Now, it's not that you're not going to give to charities, it's not that you're not going to help other people out, it's that you can't say yes every single time or your life will get sucked in.

People know that you have a sheep mentality and you have a hard time saying no. So, they'll always do what's called "The Ask." And they know that when you're down "Ask," 70% of the time or higher, you're going to get a yes, it depends on what the ask is, Why? Because people are people pleasers and there's a strong tendency towards that. This will suck up all your time. If you say yes to everybody, you're going to end up saying no to the areas, the tasks and the things that are most important to you, in life. You have to say no, or I'm out of time, or I can't help you. This is why we don't have time for our families.Because we've said yes to too many things at work. Yes to too many things that we're volunteering for.

And we forgot that, hey I married the love of my life, I raised X number of beautiful children. I said, I would do anything for them. And I was sincere when I said that. But I still want to help these other people. So, I don't realize that I'm saying yes to them ... I'm saying no to other things. We forget that every yes equals a no on the other side. Remember that and you'll save a boatload of time. You'll put your time where it's best served. Now, I'm going to share a little tip with you. Consider working for yourself. Some people call a job a J.O.B. which means 'Just Over Broke." I'll tell you, I worked for many years as a therapist, as an educator, as a trainer.

I made all the money I ever saved for retirement In about a year of working for myself. Now, I'm a five year overnight success, because it took me four years to get the formula down, but man, I made all the money, all the savings I ever had my entire life in one year of working for myself. So carefully consider this option. It's a good solid option. People say well, it's scary, what if I lose my investment? or I can't make it out? blah, blah, blah. You have no security in your job. I'm on Job number 24. Two reasons, one, businesses go out of business all the time. I've been laid off so many times, It's insane And or I went to work for a place and they were closed. So I had to find a different job.

I had to get creative, I had to go outside my field because most of the jobs were gone. I moved from New Hampshire to Florida, because most of the therapy jobs were gone. There was no place to do therapy. All the major facilities, in the 80 percentile, were gone. I even tried private practice on my own. I didn't realize those people were really just subcontracting under a business called Monadnock Family Services, and they had quote unquote "Private Practices" but they were private at all. If they don't have my Monadnock family services covering their—, 80% of their business, 80% of their expenses ... they were gone like that. I didn't do that great, I barely scraped by. But because I wasn't using Monadnock Family Services, I was crushing it compared to everybody else who was a therapist in that area of New Hampshire.

Now, Monadnock Family Services, I love them to death ... They're a great organization. They help a lot of people, please contribute to them. They're wonderful. But you've really got to work for yourself. That's the only time you have security. When you can generate an income on command, even if everything goes south. You know that you can make money, like I make money online. No matter what happens. Even if I have started from scratch, and that's happened before, I can still make money online. Why? Because I understand the fundamentals. Now, if I lose a job and there's not another job, oh my god, I've got to move out of the area.

I got to change my lifestyle. I'm working for somebody else who's making money off of me. So I'm the guy who's working for 20 bucks an hour or so, this other guy can make 3,000 dollars an hour. I mean, the formula ... but I'm on the wrong side of it. You need to get on the right side of the formula. So, work for yourself. Whether it's online, whether it's in a static business, I think that's a great idea. But you gotta be careful, because there are HIGH failure rates for new businesses. That's why I like online, even if I fail I don't have a huge investment. It's time, it's a little bit of capital, it's a little bit of education, a little bit of monthly expenses, but it's not huge. Like I put down $60,000 of my money and $180,000 dollars in somebody else's money you know, for a grand total of what like $220K. You know a quarter million dollars, boom! And if I lose it, I'm bankrupt. NO ... If I lose an online business,

I'm a couple of thousand in the hole and I start again, I start again, I start again.

I can do that several times before I go through 20 or 30 thousand. 1 out of 10, at least, is going to hit. Usually, one out of two or three and then boom! All of a sudden, I am making a hundred thousand, two hundred thousand, three hundred thousand, five hundred thousand ... a year! With a $50,000 a year job, I got to eat off at least $40,000. That's about $10,000 a year Savings It would take me 50 years to make what I can make in one year ... online. Think about it. It could be a huge time saver for you! This could be the best way to get the whole chapter. Think about it, contemplate it. See what you come up with. I can only tell you my experience. I'll see you in the next chapter.

Specific Time Management Techniques 9

Now, let's look at the staff. Here's a great question to ask yourself, "Is my staff trained in Time Management?" If not, here's the next question, ask yourself, "What the hell was I thinking?" (LOL) If I haven't trained them to save time, I'm literally asking them to waste time. ok. They can't do any better than they are trained. Why should they? How could they? It's not possible. How many things can you do, approximately, They don't know how to do? Correct answer, zero, hello, zero! You can't do better than you're trained. So don't cheat your staff. It's not their fault. They're young, they're new and sometimes even if they are old, they haven't had a Time Management chapter. You should send them to this Book. Most people haven't had even one Book in Time Management.

And if they did, only 10 percent of those who had it followed it. So, 10 percent of 10 percent is about what? 1% That's an optimistic estimate of how many of your staff, one in a hundred, have been trained and understand Time Management. It's tiny. You have to fix this. If you don't correct it, you're bleeding money. They're working on a 25 percent efficiency, when 100 percent efficiency is somewhere around about 90 percent efficiency. Nobody's perfect, but 80 to 90 percent efficiency, not 25 percent. That's where you need to get to, that's where you need to be and that is going to require what? chapter! Now, One of the first ways you can help your staff is to ask about problems.

People tend to stick their head in the sand about problems, ok. I literally use this picture. "Hear no evil, see no evil, speak no evil." People don't want to hear about problems, they just want them to go away. They don't want to see the problems. Or more aptly, they stare at the problems, not really seeing them, because if they saw me, you would think they would take care of them, right? But the difference between a blind man, and a man who won't see, is indistinguishable. And there's people that figure if we don't talk about the problem, then it isn't real. We just kind of let it chapter by, maybe it'll go away, maybe it'll "heal." No, sorry, it doesn't work that way.

So, you have to go to your staff and ask them "What do you need help with?" Matter of fact, if you brought in a genius consultant to turn around your business, do you know what they would do? They would sit down, they would interview your staff and they would ask them. "What are the problems that you currently see going on ... and what would you do about it?" And then they collect all the problems ...on one side of the ledger. Right next to it they put the answers down. They compile the biggest problems, with the best answers, and they hand it to you and you go, "Oh, my god! This is going to turn our entire company around! This is life-changing! This is amazing! How did you come up with this? You're a—genius!" Yeah, genius is the ability to check in with your

staff. (LOL) The consultants have a great model, it's kind of a great scam.

I mean, I don't I don't discount their skill. A lot of times they're brilliant in their skills and their knowledge and you know the staff doesn't always come up with the best answers, sometimes the consultant does. Sometimes the consultants have to go outside and check in with other companies. It's not quite as simple as I defined it ... but that's about 80 percent of it. Their job is 80 percent done, once they go through that process that I just shared with you. WHY don't you do that? It'll open their eyes, open their ears, when they open their mouth, perfectly. Huge Time Management Saver. Huge Money Saver.

This will even help you retain staff better, because when you actually make some of the changes that they talked about, they actually believe that you listen to them. For one logical reason, You just did! Beautiful.

Everybody wins. That's what I love. So, the next thing you need to look at, and I do this every time I go to a company, is that I have to do a turnaround. One, I did a massive chapter with the staff. Which staff? The staff that was left! I hired all the right people and I fired all the right people. Negativity was a firing offense. I got rid of them. If they weren't productive, I got rid of them. If they weren't a complete asset to that company, I said, there's somebody better out there, I'm going to find them. I'm going to hire. I'm going to raise them and train them, and get them in here.

As soon as I could get rid of somebody that wasn't performing somewhere near their peak, I got rid of them. Why should they be there? They can work for a lesser company. I'm sure a lot of lesser companies would love to have them. I'm sure they're working there now. I hear McDonald's is hiring. That's great. So ask yourself this question, "Which employees waste time or produce minimal results." So, you've got to nail this down. So, the first thing I would do is to shorten the evaluation periods. Don't do it every six months, don't do it once a year. I did them quarterly. I want to check in quarterly. Why? So, I can see how you are doing. You would get feedback sooner, which helped you as the employee. I can note progress, which means compliment you on the progress.

Or I would know you weren't making progress, and you're resistant, and it didn't take me another three months to a year to figure that out. All the while bleeding money, you were hurting my other staff, you when I was doing mental health, you were literally hurting patients. You know people that we're here to be cared for. That wasn't going to happen under my watch, under my guard, right? So, shorten evaluation periods. Help everybody. And if you need an additional chapter, you need additional help ... I know that right off. I'm getting feedback from you as well on what you need and what you've learned, and what you've run up against. You may be sincerely trying to get better and you run up against a roadblock. I found it out fairly quickly.

I even tell my staff, "Hey, I'm going to evaluate you every three months, but you can check in with me tomorrow if you hit a roadblock, don't wait till you're 90 day evaluation and say "Well, you know, I was doing great but then, this happened and kind of slowed me down." Why are you waiting somewhere between 1 and 90 and I guess 89 days to tell me this? Tell me right off. Second thing you see is "Train your staff." I already told you that's the first thing that I did ... I would Institute a chapter program. And I had tons of chapter materials on the grounds, in the facility, that people could pour through. And then I mandated certain things that I wanted them to train on.

Because again, only one in 10 when you leave the materials there or one in 20, you know somewhere between 1 percent and 10 percent usually, around five to 10, closer to 5, will ever use the chapter materials. Even though they've got everything they need right there, right in front of them, like a gold mine, to be the best in the facility, the best of the unit, to crush everybody else. They're too—lazy. Handed to them. They're too—lazy. Next, as you get rid of the negative people, one bad apple can spoil the whole bunch. The best people will leave ... when you leave the worst people in place. Get rid of them. I want to work in a place that's positive. Get rid of them.

Next, remove competition. Get people to work together. To do teamwork, Show that you value teamwork ... not you did better in your evaluation of somebody else. No, no. In the evaluations I'm asking people not only what they did, what they accomplished, and what they produced, but 'Who did you help? Who did you mentor? Who did you team with? Who did you support on your team? This was a family unit. Remove the competition ... and people won't fight each other. You don't much like your own people fighting each other. There's an old

African expression, it says, "It's easier to go in a given direction with a thousand men that want to go ... Then with one around your neck." Remove competition. Next, encourage your staff. Don't run around trying to catch people doing things wrong, run around trying to catch people doing things right.

I mean that goes way back to the "One Minute Manager, " Right? That's like an 80s, early 90s, type thing. Make that happen. So, many managers are negative, negative, negative. People will do a certain amount because there's negative pressure, and it can be very effective, but what's not worked out will be acted out. They will be more efficient ... but they will also stab you in the back every chance they can. They will let you down every chance they can. As long as it doesn't blow back on them. If there is something that will make them look bad, they don't want to bring that to you. They will hide that. That's what causes the dumb, deaf and blind, "Hear no evil, See no evil, Speak no evil." It's because management staff is being so negative.

When you encourage staff, they will help you. They will want to do the extra for you.When they probably should leave, they will stick behind you. When they could screw you ... they won't screw you. So, next, remove all the "Nega-holics". I told you that negativity was a firing offense. I worked Major hours, wherever I worked, I always put in extra time. I got paid for 40. I usually worked 50, 60 or 70. My joke was, I hated to pay my mortgage. Why? Because I visit there ... but I live here, on the job. I spend most of my waking hours with these people. So, as the boss, negativity was a firing offense, Why? Hurt the customers, or when I was doing mental health that hurt the clients, it hurt the other people I worked with, and somebody else I care about ... ME! I didn't want to work with negative people.

And negative people are up to 50 percent less effective than positive people! And you know what? You leave one negative person around five positive people and they will drop the other five people's productivity anywhere from 10 to 30 percent. So, an average of 20 to 25 percent. So, if you're a negative person and you're in a team of five people, you're dropping other people's productivity, say 20-25 percent, you are virtually costing me in productivity when I pay you! I could have those four people alone in a room by themselves and produce almost as much as all five of you together or the same. And they would be happier doing it. So, no matter how valuable a negative person was, I got rid of him as quickly as I could.

Unless it was a deal breaker. They were like CFO, I needed them to do the books. You know, I would keep them there JUST long enough to replace them. Everybody else, Boom! So, as I found out you were negative, you were damaging the work other people were doing, you were hurting customers or clients. Bam! You were gone so fast, it would make your head spin! And I would make sure that EVERYBODY knew, you were gotten rid of because you are that wildly negative And that anybody wants to be that negative, they're next. And this is going to be a positive place. And all the right people love that philosophy, and all the right people hate that philosophy. All the positive people were thrilled.

"Thank God, you got here! You know, three other management teams left that person here that made my life, my very existence, almost intolerable. Can't believe they kept them. You finally got rid of them and I know you're not going to let negative people in. I'm going to stay here until you or I die, because now I've got a positive work environment. You know how rare that is?" Your staff will LOVE you! Next, Increase Staff Resources. Starting with the chapter materials, but also other things they need. There's a lot of things that aren't chapter issues. They're not attitudinal issues, like the negativity. They are RESOURCE issues. People simply don't have the things that they need.

The simple things that they need to be productive, So, that's basically how you look at it, how you handle it and how you deal with the staff. If you follow these guidelines, Think of what you can end up with ... You're going to end up with staff that knows exactly how they're doing. They're never nervous about their job. They're very well-trained. They know if they stay with you, they're going to continue to get wiser and they're going to grow in their job. That's going to keep people there. They know that they're going to progress in their job. They know they're going to make more money, because as they make me more money, I pay them more money. Hello? I pay them more money! I bring them along with me. "A rising tide raises all boats." They're going to be in a positive work environment and they're not going to struggle to have what they want. And they're going to have that work environment that they always wanted.

And I tell you the older staff gets, and the more valuable they get, the more they care about quality of life. What does it FEEL like when I'm at work? Not what are my benefits? what's my package? and what's my pay? and you know, where can I go? Do I FEEL GOOD at my job? That's what they want! Give them that, give them a home. They will love you, they will protect you, they will become family. They will do the extra for you. Productivity will go through the roof. You'll be happier, they'll be happier and it will be a win, win, win, win, win, win, win. You will absolutely, positively, crush it. Think about that. Enjoy that. That's a positive message for you and I'll see you in the next and final chapter. Congratulations!

Effective Time Management - Conclusion & Final Thoughts

Hey, welcome back. You are one of my favorite people in the world. That is not an overstatement. You know why? Because there's not one person in a 100 that will take a Book like this. And then about 75 to 80 percent of people will not get through to the end. This puts you in the top 20 percent of the top 1 percent that make things happen! I love people that start things, and be in a sound mind ,when they have great material in front of them, they finish it. Do you know that's actually the rarest thing in the world? People say, I wish I had an advantage. I wish I had a way to get ahead. No, they don't! They've AVOIDED so many ways to get ahead. Look at all the chapters that are out there. People are begging you to go to school, take a Book, read a book. There's so much great information out there and rarely, if ever, is it consumed.

Do you know that over 90 percent of the books sold from Barnes and Noble, people think their intellectual, their readers, are all basically soft—, they're dramas and mostly women reading romance novels. Literally crap! Or things on stamp collecting, and junk like that, is a big part of the other 10 percent. It's like 1 percent to 2 percent is actually "How do I get out there ... How do I make my life better? How do I become a better employee? How do I become more healthy? How do I have better time management? How do I get better at my job? How am I a better parent, better friend, better brother, sister, lover, whatever, in some way shape or form, self improvement. And then actually take the information home ... and finish it. That is exceedingly rare! It boggles the mind, but it's exceedingly rare, wildly rare, 1 percent, quarter of 1 percent. It is so easy to be the best in almost any industry ... because so many people are lying down on the job.

They call them "RIP" which means "Rest In Place", in business, it means "Retired In Place." (LOL) They are never going to move! They've already quit. It might be day one ... most people are "retired in place." You're just going to try to get by. But YOU are the exemplar, you are the person making it happen, You are crushing it! OH MY GOD, I AM SO PROUD OF YOU! You're amazing! So, I want to wrap this up. Last tips. Make time management part of the employee evaluations. That's what we talked about in the last chapter. Make sure you're shortening the time in which we do evaluations.

Now, we're talking about what we do inside of those evaluations, specifically to Time Management. Make SURE that you make Time Management part of the evaluation. I don't know why this isn't measured in evaluations. It's one of the key things. I pay you an hourly wage which means I pay you for your time. Then I get to the evaluation and I don't measure how you use that time. Oh my God! Are people high? Is management high? Is HR high? Are the corporations high? When they're making out these evaluation forms ... that they don't try to see how you're using your time? That's insane! But there it is. Don't do this in your evaluations, don't do this when you're the boss. Certainly, do not do this inside your company.

This is why so many businesses fail. So, one tip I want to share with you too, from Edwards Deming. Deming is actually the Deming award. The Deming Award ... they give that over in Asia. Strange thing, that's how they did "The Asian Turnaround." They listened to Edward Deming, he was our best and brightest mind for how to be productive. And he simply stated, "What doesn't get measured doesn't get done." So, make sure when you give people assignments, you've got measurements, you've got touchstones, different time dates, when things are supposed to be done. Check it along the way, not, I gave this to you today, 90 days later it's done. Most people will jump in saying, hey in only a week or two left, 10 days left, five days left, three days left.

Do you have this done? And it's nothing like 90 percent done, It's nothing like 50 percent done And it's crunch time, this is procrastination. Because you're not measuring it, you're not checking in. Always measure, always check in, always evaluate, always praise, always guide, always give the extra resources that people need. Find out problems early. In therapy we used to say, "There's a time in the life of every problem when it's big enough to see ... but small enough to deal with easily." That's what you ought to be doing. Measure, check in. But be sure to make Time Management a key component of employee evaluations. You'll be glad you did. Now, one of the great Time Management tips is simply to develop a "Time Management Mindset." Whatever you focus on, you get better at.

So, you want to have a time management mindset. Always thinking, how can I save more time, how can I save more time, how can I save more time? There's actually a part of your brain, an interesting psychological fact, it's called the "Reticular Activator." Whatever you focus on you'll find, because your reticular activity will start scanning the environment and find the resources you need to meet the goal that you keep in the front of your mind. So, if you have a Time Management Mindset and you're always looking for ways to save time, your reticular activator will scan the environment. It will find ways that you can save time.

It'll put that in the front of your brain, instead of hiding it in the back of your brain. You will gather new ways to save time. You'll become a time master, a master of time. And you will have mastery in time management. Just what we promised you at the beginning of this program, right? This will take you 80 or 90 percent of the way to Time Mastery Management. It doesn't take you 100 percent of the way. Why? Because there's thousands of ways to save time. We have given you the core competencies. And a lot of the very unique competencies that you never, ever, ever, see in a Time Management book or chapter.

I saw a Time Management book ... It was done by Yale or Harvard, one of the major Ivy League universities.

It was this tiny book and it was probably about maybe 90 pages long ... and it was pure crap! By the best and the brightest, it was pure crap. I looked at these time management techniques and I said to myself, "I can do at least that bad." (LOL) It was like a $35 book. This was an expensive hardcover book, and I'm like, this is rubbish. I would throw this right in the trash! Over 90 pages, there's four good ideas in here. And they were so basic, I'd be embarrassed to put them in a book on Time Management. I said, "I can crush these guys." I can crush these guys in the first 10 pages. So, I created my own Time Management book, which bits and pieces are found in here. Ultimately, I'll publish the whole book.

I'm not done yet. Like I said there's hundreds and hundreds of different ways, that are good solid ways, major ways ,that most people can use to save time. When I get all of those together, and I get enough time, I'm going to put together a book on Time Management ... and put that out there. But for now, I'd rather get the best of the best out there to you, right now. So, I want you to go out there and I want you to have that mindset. You can gather ways to save time. Specific to your needs, your focus, your business and your future. I want you to have the best future ever! Let me leave you with this thought, "Time cannot be replaced." Write that down. Time cannot be replaced. I love this quote.

It's by Samuel Smiles. It says, "Lost wealth may be replaced by industry, lost knowledge by study, lost health by temperance or medicine, but lost time is gone forever." So, you have any questions? I'm not sure which platform you're buying this through. I have multiple platforms. People are just dying to get my materials. But if you have questions, I always wanna answer them for you. I'll get back to you as soon as I can. I'm a very busy man ... but not too busy that I don't have what? Time for you! :) So, if you have any questions go ahead whatever portole you're in, whatever educational system you bought this through, message me, I will get back to you as soon as I can. I love you for finishing this Book. I love you for having the questions and wanting to do better, desiring to do better and making the effort to do better.

You know many times you're successful when you are, when you do that? 99.9%. I think in the future, You're going to be massively successful. My name is Professor . I want to thank you so much for joining us today. You've been a wonderful student, you've been a great audience and I really appreciate you. I'm there for you and I hope to see you in my next Book.

Don't miss out!

Visit the website below and you can sign up to receive emails whenever SHAKRUDDIN KHAN publishes a new book. There's no charge and no obligation.

https://books2read.com/r/B-A-DUGBB-QEAYC

BOOKS 2 READ

Connecting independent readers to independent writers.

Also by SHAKRUDDIN KHAN

The Smart Way To Personal Finance Success
Goal Setting 101 Achieve More Goals Than Ever! Faster!
Blockchain Masterclass for Businesses and Corporations
Master Your Mindset & Brain Framestorm Your Way To Success
Manipulation Techniques: How Can We Influence People's Thoughts
And Behaviors
Leadership How To Influence, Inspire And Impact As A Leader
Learn How To Create A Safe Working Environment For Your Team